THE CHRISTIANITY OF JESUS CHRIST
Is it Ours?

By
MARK GUY PEARSE
Author of **Thoughts on Holiness**

Revised and Edited by David N. Bubar

**The Christianity of Jesus Christ,
Is It Ours?**
Author, Mark Guy Pearse
Revised and Edited by David N. Bubar
Copyright 2002.

ISBN1-885273-11-8
First Century Publishing
P.O. Box 130
Delmar, NY 12054
1-800-578-6060 Fax: (518) 439-0105
www.firstcenturypublishing.com

CONTENTS

About the Author
Mark Guy Pearse

Mark Guy Pearse, a Methodist theologian and writer, was born March 1, 1842 in Camborne, England. As a young man, he attended school in Camborne and Holland. He later went on to study medicine at Wesley College and worked at St. Bartholomew's Hospital in London.

His career path took a different course, however, when in 1863 he became a Methodist clergyman. Pearse discovered his divine inspiration listening to the sermons of Methodist minister Charles Hadden Spurgeon. They became friends and Pearse assisted Spurgeon with his missionary works in Leeds, Ipswich, Bedford, Westminister and Bristol. In 1899, in connection with the West London Mission, Pearse became an active missionary to St. James Hall where he remained for fourteen years.

The conditions of the poor and destitute in 1899 industrial London were appalling to Rev. Pearse. People who were out of work and unable to find steady jobs and wages watched helplessly while their families starved. The workhouses or sweatshops were hardly a solution, as they would surely break up the family by branding them paupers.

The typical wage was five shillings a week for twelve to fourteen hours of hard labor in the sweatshops every day. Pearse once said of those who attended church and prayer meetings, but refused to address the social evils existing all around them, "If this is Christianity, the sooner we get rid of Christianity, the better."

Equally as disturbing to Pearse, were those fortunate enough to have steady work and could support thier families, but were led astray by alcohol abuse. Men would spend all of their time and wages in pubs while their families looked on, helpless against their savage addiction. Pearse viewed the liquor industry as being the culprit behind many of the domestic and economic hardships of the working class.

In 1884 Pearse published *The Story of Billy Bray*, which is the tale of a miner who resorts to sin, carnality and drunkenness. His wife is forced to fetch him each night out of the local pubs. However, one day Billy is given a book to read. The title is *Visions of Heaven and Hell* by John Bunyan. Its contents have a profound and enlightening effect on Billy. He is reborn and, having discovered his salvation, is ready to serve God at all cost.

As in *The Story of Billy Bray*, *The Christianity of Jesus Christ, Is It Ours?* conveys a similar message. It is Christ's invitation to the weary and the heavy-laden. The reader will ultimately realize that he or she is the "ye" *"who shall receive power after that the Holy Ghost is come upon you, and ye shall be witnesses unto me."* (Acts 1:18)

Introduction

While on Earth, Jesus Christ gave, taught, practiced, lived and demonstrated a way of life that changed our world. For over 2000 years His teachings have been proclaimed on planet Earth. Controversy, confusion, finger-pointing, accusations, and almost every emotion known to man has abounded among those claiming to be Christians, and who consider their own personal flavor of Christianity to be the true Christianity.

What has happened to the Christianity of past ages that was listened to, transforming lives and giving healing through its message, and where people used their powerful and fearless Christian faith to do great things for the Creator; founding nations, such as the United States of America, and were not ashamed of their Christian faith, or to be called Christians?

What is the true Christianity of Jesus Christ as taught by Jesus Christ? Is it locked up in a particular denomination, religion or religious group as some claim? Why have many of the once respected "mainline" Christian denominations that once demonstrated the power of Jeus Christ now lost their power and have declined to become merely "side-line" denominations and religions? Does the true Christianity elect one to Heaven and eject another to hell? Which religious group has the true Christianity?

Is the true Christianity given by Jesus Christ not powerful enough to attract people without "religious entertainment," and having to get all "psyched up" in order to worship Him? Are there many different types of Christianity--or just one? Is it necessary to "take up your cross and follow me," "feed my sheep," and to "go out in the highways and byways" in order to practice the true Christianity taught by Christ?

And what about those who claim to be Christians, but are dishonest in their business dealings, have no joy or peace in their lives; and act, dress and live like the so-called heathens, or the non-Christians?

In this book, Mark Guy Pearse makes it very clear what Jesus Christ taught and established with the church He founded in the First Century. It may be a different brand of Christianity which you practice. Read on and decide for yourself--*The Christianity of Jesus Christ, Is It Ours?*

David N. Bubar, Editor.

Chapter I

CHRIST'S IDEA OF CHRISTIANITY

The many aspects in which Christianity presents itself may perhaps be summed up in these three:

First. "It is a revelation of God, and of our relation to Him".

Second. "It is a means of individual salvation."

Third. "It is the power of God for conquering and regenerating the world."

Of these, the first and second are constantly kept to the front. But without the third the other two must ever be incomplete. The evils which those within the church most deeply deplore, and which the foes of Christ fasten upon most readily for criticism and scorn, spring from the neglect of the great purpose of Christianity in relation to the world. Unless it be accepted in the completeness of Christ's claims and purposes, our religion may only perpetuate and intensify the very evils for which

He came to remedy. The urgency of the appeal to men to seek their own salvation, the promises of religion for this world and for the world to come, can scarcely fail to minister to our very selfishness, unless we go on to learn our responsibility in reference to the world's conversion. We cannot fully realize any of the blessings of Christianity unless they flow out of us to bless the world. We cannot know truly the fatherhood of God except as it leads us into a true brotherliness toward all men. The salvation that is in Jesus Christ is ours exactly in proportion as we die to ourselves and live to the glory of God and the good of others. We trace Christianity to its spring and source, and find it in the heart of the Eternal Father: *"God so loved the world, that he gave his only begotten son."* (John. 3:16). There is the manner and the measure of the Father's love and wherever that love dwells it must shape itself after the pattern seen in the mount.

The Apostle John becomes again the indignant *"Son of Thunder"* at the thought of any manifestation of religion that stops short of this. *"If a man say , I love God, and hateth his brother, he is a liar: for he that loveth not his brother whom he hath seen, how can he love God whom he hath not seen?"* (1 John. 4:20). Loved with a love so wonderful, redeemed at a cost so priceless, there is but one proof of our love that will suffice; what is it? *"Hereby perceive we the love of God, that He laid down His life for us."* (1 John. 3:16), that we accept and rest in; but the claim which grows out of that love, alas! We are slow to admit — *"We ought to lay down our lives for the brethren"* (1 John. 3:16).

Of that we stop short. We accept the love of God; we accept the gift of salvation; but of the third great purpose of religion, a power in us for the conversion of the world, we are content to remain in untroubled ignorance. This is the great hindrance to Christianity — un-Christ-like Christians. To uplift and purify the religion of our time; to put into it the heroism and might of a conquering force, it is needful for us to search out Christ's idea of Christianity, and then with all our hearts to give ourselves up to it.

This purpose of God in giving his Son, the purpose of Jesus Christ our Savior in all his life and death and resurrection; and the purpose of the Holy Spirit in every breath of his influence within the Church is one — the salvation of the world. We are "of God" only as this purpose possesses us, and directs and controls our whole life.

Upon what, then, does the salvation of the world depend?

There are abundant promises which speak of the kingdoms of the world becoming the kingdoms of Christ — promises that the earth shall be full of the knowledge of the Lord as the waters cover the sea. *"He must reign until he hath put all enemies under his feet."* (1 Corinthians 15: 25) These glorious events shine ever before us — the Church's hope, joy and strength. From age to age the conviction abides that as the Almighty Father made the world, as the Son of God redeemed it, so assuredly the Holy Ghost is come to regenerate the world and to fill it with the glory of God.

But how is the work to be done? Churches and varied church arrangements, preachers, and workers of all sorts, are more plentiful than ever before. Yet who of us is content with the progress of the gospel? Is this country of ours a model of what Christianity can make of a nation? — its pride, its love of money, its haste and eagerness to be rich at any cost, and by any means? If this is all that Christianity can do for us, is it really worthwhile to go to the trouble of training men and sending them, at much expense, to the ends of the earth? Or, if there is a power that can cast out these devils, what is it? Where is it? Why is it not felt and seen?

Our hopes and our despair, our faith and our fears, may drive us honestly and earnestly to search into Christ's idea of Christianity. If it is the divine plan for the world's salvation, why does it seem to fail in its purpose? Is it lacking in power, or is it wrongly applied? These are the questions which press upon us, demanding an answer.

Let us begin at the Acts of the Apostles, carefully looking at the first chapter, where the history of the church commences.

"*The former treatise have I made, O Theophilus, of all that Jesus began both to do and to teach.*" (Acts 1:1). So Luke begins his second book. Very notable is that word "*began.*"

It is not the word that would ever be used of any other man when he was dead and buried — "*Of all that he began to do and to teach.*" Whatever they may have been, when men go down into the grave their doing and teaching are over, though their influence may abide. But this was a beginning on each until the day in which he was taken up. So then, Christianity is that same Christ going on doing, and teaching, only in a new condition, he is now the risen Christ; and in a new method through the church which is his body.

"*After that he through the Holy Ghost had given commandments unto the apostles whom he had chosen.*" (Acts 1:2b)

Again a strange saying, "*Through the Holy Ghost had given commandments.*" Had not Christ authority to say to one, go, and he goeth, and to another, come, and he cometh? Here is at once a great mystery and a simple fact. What the Holy Spirit did for the Lord Jesus we know not, but the result and outcome of the Holy Spirit's work is most manifest. The record of it is from the pen of Luke, and his Gospel enables us to see of what he is thinking as he writes these words: "*And Jesus returned in the power of the Spirit into Galilee . . . And he came to Nazareth, where he had been brought up; and, as his custom was, he went into the synagogue on the Sabbath Day, and stood up for to read.*" (Luke 4:14 & 4:16).

Now, if there was any place where they knew the Lord Jesus, it was in this village of Nazareth. Everybody knew him. He had grown up amongst them. He was one of them. But this day they turned to each in wonder, almost in doubt, asking, "*Is not this Joseph's son?*" (Luke 4:6). None but gracious words ever came from those lips, but they never heard words like these. They marveled; their eyes were fastened upon him. A force was amongst them such as they had never felt before. It was the power of the Holy Ghost.

Let us notice very carefully the lines that are thus laid down from the beginning of the Christian Church. Jesus Christ accepted exactly our human conditions of service, and wrought only in the same power as that which was to be the strength of his church. This is his starting point, and here his great work begins — *"Jesus being full of the Holy Ghost."* (Luke 4:1). Then the temptation follows immediately, for it finds its whole meaning and stress in the condition of service which Christ has accepted. It is a very shallow thought of the temptation which sees it only as having reference to Christ's hunger. It was the meeting between the Prince of this world, who claims authority over it, and the new man, the Second Adam, to whom was given dominion over the earth to subdue it. The temptation turned upon the method by which the victory was to be won. It was no triumph that God in his omnipotence should defeat any creature, though it was the fallen archangel. That had already been done. But that man Christ Jesus, with no other force than that which all men could share, go forth to destroy the dominion of Satan — this was a humiliation which the proud prince of hell might well dread, and a conflict for which he could gather his forces with some hope of victory. So the tempter draws near. *"If thou be the Son of God, command that these stones be made bread."* (Matthew 4:3). Let not thine omnipotence lie unused, lest indeed it be unacknowledged. For thy bodily need, and to preserve thy life for thy great work, put forth thy Divine power — over men, of course. Thy control is to be moral only and spiritual but, here are these stones — coarse material upon which thou canst indulge thy power and relieve thy want. Very notable is the first word of that Scripture which Jesus quotes in reply — *"It is written, Man"* (Matthew 4:7) — He had been addressed as the Son of strength, but answered with the sword of the Spirit.

Then comes the second temptation — very subtle it is. *"If thou be the Son of God,"* (Matthew 4:6) show that thy faith in God is sublime. Let a weak, doubting world see how faith like thine fears nothing, knows no peril. Put forth a superhuman trust to teach men trust — a Godlike faith, that men may believe in it. Again the quotation of a Scripture taken to himself, and used for his defense, which has reference to poor Israel.

Then came the third temptation. "Well, thou art going forth as a man to thy work. The kingdoms of the world are mine. Thou wilt have to win them back by shame, by misery, by agony and bloody sweat and awful death upon the cross. Against thee shall be arrayed all the principalities and powers of earth and hell. Thy followers shall suffer as thou dost; and through all the ages thou wilt have to reckon with me. See now, they are at thy feet — the kingdoms of the world and the glory of them. They are mine. Think of thyself. Think of thy followers. Think of the good thou couldst accomplish so easily and swiftly and certainly. If the world were thine, and the glory, how couldst thou end its woes, and wipe away its tears, and fill it with thy glory! I can give it to whom I will. It is thine — all thine — if for one single moment thou wilt acknowledge my authority over it."

And there it lay — the world within his grasp; so easily won, so cheaply and the other way so long, so dark, so dreadful — the way of the cross and the grave! It was a splendid triumph when Jesus Christ, the Holy Ghost, waved it all aside, and bade Satan begone: "*For it is written, thou shalt worship the Lord thy God, and him only shalt thou serve.*" (Matthew 4:10). This was the lifelong temptation of Christ, gathering its most dreadful force when he hung despised and rejected on the cross, and about him broke the storm of taunts — "*Let him save himself*" — "*Come down from the cross.*" (Matthew 27:40). To be possessed of omnipotence, and yet to pass with such desires amidst such needs; to have such power in the face of such foes, and yet always to accept the human conditions of service — this was the sublime triumph of the Son of Man. He is the human agent filled with the Holy Ghost. Miracles were wrought by this same power of the Holy Ghost. He himself announces this as the source of his strength, and the fitness for his work:

"*And when he had opened the book, he found the place where it was written: The Spirit of the lord is upon me, because he had anointed me to preach the gospel to the poor; he had sent me to heal the brokenhearted, to preach deliverance to the captives, and recovering of sight to the blind, to set at liberty them that are bruised, to proclaim the acceptable year of the Lord.*" (Luke 4:18-19).

This is the great root idea of Christianity — men and women carrying on Christ's work, living over again Christ's life in the power which fitted him for his service — the power of the Holy Ghost. Miracles are to be wrought, not for the Church from without, but by the Church from within. God could bring all men instantly to their knees in lowliest submission before him; earthquakes, flashing meteors, great wants and perils from which prayer brought miraculous deliverance, should speedily secure that. But this cuts across the condition laid down by Christ from the first. The power which is to transform the world is from within men, and not from without. The Spirit of God dwelling in Jesus Christ, and filling him with power — this is the starting point of Christianity.

And now, in all the consciousness of what the Holy Spirit did for him, the Lord Jesus speaks to his disciples: "*And being assembled together commanded them that they should not depart from Jerusalem, but wait for the promise of the Father, which, saith he, Ye have heard of me. For John truly baptized with water, but ye shall be baptized with the Holy Ghost not many days hence.*" (Acts 1:5).

The mention of "*days*" seemed at once to define the restoration of that little Jewish kingdom to which their hopes were still limited.

"*When they therefore were come together, they asked of him, saying, Lord, wilt thou at this time restore again the kingdom of Israel? and he said, it is not for you to know times or seasons, which the Father hath set within his own authority.*" (Acts 1:7).

Surely it were well to heed these words of our Master. If we could know the times or seasons, it were better we should not, since he has spoken thus. What business have we to be prying into secrets of which the Lord has said it is not for us to know them? The Master means us to spend all our time in doing something every way better. If we had lived before Christ's coming, who of us would not have longed to be a prophet; to climb the hill, and watch through the darkness for the first faint streak that told of His coming day? But now every one of us has a grander work to do than that of any prophet that ever lived. Nobler and more glorious than Isaiah, or Elijah, or Moses, is the calling and purpose of every Christian — he that is least in the kingdom of heaven is greater than these. Ours it is, not to point into the hazy distance, and tell of a Christ that is coming. Ours it is to be filled with the Holy Ghost, and to let men see a Christ that is come. Witnesses — not prophets; this is our high calling.

But what concerns us most is the other part of the question and the answer. *"Lord, wilt thou bring back to thyself the kingdoms of the world?"* (Acts 1:6). This was in effect the question, and thus we may put it. Here about their Master cluster the eager disciples — "WILT THOU?" thou hast triumphed over all foes, over Roman and Pharisee, over Death and Hell; and, now thou art come forth in the power of thy resurrection — wilt thou not complete thy triumph and subdue thine enemies? Thus the Church ever stands, looking up with longing and wonder — "Lord, wilt thou save the world? Wilt thou assert thine authority, and bring the nations to thyself?"

What is the answer, the answer for all the ages? Jesus bent over them and said, "Ye." They looked up; he looked down. They thought it all rested with him — and he laid that work upon them. *"Ye — Ye shall receive power after that the Holy Ghost is come upon You, and Ye shall be witnesses unto me."* (Acts 1:8).

Then, as if there were nothing more to be said or done, while they beheld, he was taken up; and a cloud received him out their sight.

"*Ye*" — there it all rested henceforth. *"Ye shall receive power."* It is a word differing from that in the previous verse, which is also rendered *power* — that is, *authority*. This is force — dynamite if you will; for the very word has of late been brought into our language.

If there is one word that sums up Christ's idea of Christianity as revealed in the Gospels and in the Acts of the Apostles, it is this word *power*. The word is ever associated with the Holy Ghost. After the resurrection, when Christ declares that all power is given to him, the word used is authority, that is, power when it is declared and acknowledged. Such is the triumph in which Christ's work ends. But the power in which he goes forth to his work is this force. This was *"the power of the Spirit"* (Romans 15: 19) in which he returned to Nazareth. It is the word used by Christ when he declared that virtue had gone out of him. The rendering in the New Version is much more vigorous — *"perceiving in himself that the power proceeding from him had gone forth."* (Mark 1:27). Christ did not only found a new philosophy; he brought into the world a force to destroy the works of the devil. Christianity is not only a theory or a revelation; it is a transforming might in the midst of men. It is not only a method of individual salvation; it is a power by which the kingdoms of this world are to be brought back to their rightful owner. Christ was not only the teacher of a loftier morality; but *"with authority and power he commanded the unclean spirits, and they came out."* (Mark 1:27).

And now taking up the word again, he declares to the company of believers which constituted the Church — *"Ye shall receive power after the Holy Ghost is come upon you, and ye shall be witnesses unto me."* (Acts 1:8). This power was to come upon them and thus should the kingdom be restored to the God of Israel. This, and this only, is the essential of Christianity as a conquering power in the world. Christianity began with the incarnation — God in man; and this is the con-

tinuance of Christianity—God manifest in the flesh—
men and women filled with the Spirit of God. Everything without this avails nothing. Having this, everything else will follow.

Look at it. Think of it. A hundred and twenty
men and women, having no patronage, no promise of
any earthly favor; no endowment, no wealth — a company of men and women having to get their living by
common daily toil, and busied with all the household
duties of daily life — and yet they are to begin the con-
quests of Christianity! To them is entrusted a work
which is to turn the world upside down! None so exalted but the influence of this lowly company shall reach
to them, until the throne of the Caesar's is claimed for
Christ. None so far off but the power of this little band
gathered in an upper room shall extend to them, until
the world is knit into a brotherhood! Not a force is
there on the earth, either of men or devils, but they
shall overcome it, until every knee shall bow to their
Master, and every tongue shall confess that he is Lord.
(Isaiah 45:23; Romans. 14:11; Phil. 2:10). A thing impossible, absurd, look at it as you will, until you admit
this — they are to be filled with the Holy Ghost. Then
the difficulties melt into the empty air. Then there is
no limit to their hopes, for there is no limit to their
power. Their strength is not only "as strength of ten;"
it is as the strength of the Almighty. This is Christ's
idea of Christianity; the idea not of man — it is infinitely too sublime — the idea of God.

Chapter II

OUR IDEA OF CHRISTIANITY: MEN AND METHODS

So then the work of the world's salvation is to be wrought through us. How do we today accept the charge? Had we been in the place of the early church we probably would have appointed a committee or council, consisting of a dozen of the most influential men, to consider the matter; and so at the very outset we would have transferred the interest and the responsibility from the whole church to "the executive." Then after many meetings and much delay, during which the oldest members of the little company would probably have passed away, we would at last be ready to present a list of suggestions and recommendations something like these:

1. That the more gifted among the disciples be set apart for this work and proceed at once to be trained and thoroughly qualified.

2. That after such training, those who understand how to reach the people, and can adopt the right methods, be accordingly sent forth.

3. That it is very desirable, so far as possible, to secure men whose hearts are filled with enthusiasm for the work, and that their motives be pure and unselfish.

4. That in every case it is essential that those who take part in this work have due authority, that they be ordained and set apart for it.

If each and all of these requirements are secured, and these conditions are complied with, we are warranted in expecting great results.

Go over these resolutions, and see if they are not thoroughly orthodox. Do they not set forth all that we consider essential for the conquest of the world by the church? Orthodox, yes, but the whole spirit and purpose of them is utterly removed from the idea of Christianity which Christ laid down. We select and set apart men, and they are to take upon themselves the responsibility which the Lord Jesus Christ has laid upon the whole church. We expect, or at any rate we desire, that the pastor should be filled with the Holy Ghost, but as for the congregation — well, it would be a good thing, but by no means of so much importance. Christ promises the gift to all and requires it of all. For the sake of organization it may be needful that there be superintendents, and that the women as well as the men, and each went forth alike entrusted with the work of the Lord Jesus Christ, alike responsible for overcoming the world and for establishing his kingdom here on earth. This is the first great departure from the Christianity of Christ.

The disciples of old time looked up to the Lord and said, "*Wilt thou restore again the kingdom?*" (Acts 1:6b). The church today does not look so high as that — it looks to the pastor, and thinks that it is his work, and he ought to do it. We have thrust the pastor altogether out of his position. "*Ye are the light of the world*" (Matthew 5:14), Christ told to all his disciples. The pastor is not the golden candlestick, stately and prominent, diffusing illumination; rather, his emblem is in the golden snuffers keeping all the lights bright and shining. Christ puts the work of the world's conversion upon the whole church. But for the great body of Christians — Christianity is no longer a power by which they are to conquer the world for the Lord Jesus, it has become a pleasant arrangement by which they may find their way leisurely to heaven, anything further is not their department, it belongs to the pastors at home and abroad, and their duty ends with their annual subscription.

Look again at the conditions which the church of today considers essential to the triumph of Christianity over the world. Yet, the early church had all these qualifications and more than will ever be the case again; but, the Lord Jesus told the disciples to wait.

Think of the immense and unequaled advantages which these men possessed. Is the triumph of Christianity dependent upon men who are duly qualified and rightly trained? The Lord himself, who knoweth the hearts of all men, chose these. He himself was their Professor of Divinity. They sat at his feet and learned of him. What training could have any to equal this?

To have been with him, to have seen him day after day, to have heard His expounding the Word, to have gone in and out with him — of all gifts and advantages surely this was the greatest.

How vividly they could tell of him. Their memories treasured his utterances in his very tones! And they had seen with their own eyes his marvelous deeds! As they spoke of him, they could not fail to catch something of his look, his manner, his spirit. How powerfully could they preach the gospel, to whom it was not a bare statement of events, but an experience throbbing with life! That great example was ever before them. His image was graven on their minds and hearts. They knew him, not by an occasional visit, but by those years of daily, hourly fellowship and close friendship. Never again can any be trained as these had been, they were indeed doctors of divinity. And yet these were the men who were to wait for the power from on high before taking the Gospel before the world.

Is the triumph of Christianity then to be secured by right methods? These men knew the methods of their Master. Whatever there may be in successful methodology they knew. Trained not as we train men, by making theology a matter of intellectual analysis and arrangement, but by direct and constant contact with people with every variety of character. They were trained as doctors are trained, by dealing with the men and women whom they had to understand and to whom they had to minister — trained by the Great Physician himself. Who can ever have opportunity and advantage like they had? They observed daily the service and ministry of Jesus. They saw first hand his treatment of the good and the sinful, of the wise and the foolish, of the haughty Pharisee and the lowly publican, of the scornful scribe and the outcast sinner, of the sad and the suffering, of all sorts and conditions of men. If right methods would secure the triumph of Christianity, these men were prepared to go forth, for they were indeed trained well. But these are they to whom Christ said *"wait."*

Is the triumph of the church a matter secured by the authority of the pastors? Is the needful power a matter of orders? Is it true then, that if the pastor be rightly ordained, that success is secured? Never again can there be such assured authority as there was in the early church — people called, commissioned, authorized, and ordained by the Lord Jesus Christ himself, the head of the church. Yet they were told to wait. Neither their position nor their titles availed them anything; they had to sit still because there was more. *"Wait,"* said the Master, and wait they did, tarrying at Jerusalem. The Lord told them they would receive power that was not an earthly power. *"Ye shall receive power after that the Holy Ghost is come upon you"* (Acts 1:8).

Training, method, motive and authority may be worth much after men have received the power from on high; but without it, all these are nothing.

Chapter III

OUR IDEA OF CHRISTIANITY: MONEY

Let us turn again to the little company of men and women into whose hands had been entrusted this great work of restoring the kingdoms of the world to Christ. We cannot pretend for a moment that the conditions which have been suggested as essential to the success of such a work would be the only conditions named. There are needs very much less spiritual that would occur to most of us if we were entrusted with a work so vast and so far reaching. The first thought of our practical twenty-first century would be this — the need for a great deal of money.

And if we were as poor as that little company of men and women to whom Christ spoke, what consternation and despair would come upon us as to the money! Where will it come from? If we open a subscription list we might perhaps get Joseph of Arimathea to head it; but as for us, we can do nothing!

"We will need a great deal of money" — what a familiar sound the phrase has! How natural it seems and how necessary! We measure our possibilities for the world's conversion by our money. It is the sum of our wants. The cry of the church is, give, give, give; and the dream of the zealous is of the wonderful works they could do if only they had the money.

Now let us ask ourselves earnestly, Why is it that in the beginning of this great commission not a single word about money was ever spoken, either by the Master or by the disciples? If money is essential to this work, why did not Jesus Christ secure it for himself when he went forth, and in turn secure a vast endowment for his disciples at the commencement of their work? Did he not know how much of the energy and heart and time of the church would be crippled and hampered, and her work sometimes actually given up, for want of money? And yet he does not say one word about it. And when a very rich man comes to him one day, he quietly bids him go and get rid of his money and then come and follow him. What does it mean? There is a vague impression that in those times of intense spirituality and sweet simplicity, they somehow managed without money. If that be so, then, in the name of the Lord Jesus Christ, let us strive to get back to such a blessed condition. They needed money as much as we do, but they had a great deal less of it. How is it then, that the early church did not seem to have felt the need of that which is the supreme requisite of the church today? Christianity, as we see it in the New Testament, has no more to do with tithes than with incense or ephods. Jesus Christ gave no command or promise about money, except, that he told his disciples to provide neither gold nor silver nor brass in their purse as they went about witnessing.

"But we must have money of course," says everybody, as if that ended all question, and as if everything must stand still until the money is given. Faith, boldness, and sacrifice for the Lord Jesus, are all to be suppressed until the tithes are in the storehouse; then go forth and be as bold as you please, only be very careful not to step beyond the funds at hand. It is, of course, very easy to sneer at all this and say it is a little matter. The question is, did the Lord Jesus Christ intend the success and triumph of the church to depend in any degree upon money? *"Ye shall receive power, after that the Holy Ghost is come upon you."* (Acts 1:8). Is this condition dependent in the slightest degree upon the income of the church? And yet we all declare that we must have money. Do we really mean to assert that we believe in a system to evangelize the whole world, and that its great founder and head has all power in heaven and in earth, and yet his church is perpetually on the point of failure for want of money? If we must have money, if money is essential for the triumph of Christianity, let us have the confidence to go to God and ask for it, and let us have the assurance that it will be given. Better in every way to give up all faith than to believe that God so loved the world that he gave his only son, and then that he should let the world's conversion stand still for want of money. *"The gold is mine, saith the Lord of hosts."* (Haggai 2:8) He needs no beggars. He depends on no man's gifts. The fact is that there is not money enough in the world to hire men to do this work, and there never will be. When the Lord Jesus laid this work upon the whole church, he arranged it in such a way that no other method can ever succeed. Surely, nothing can be further from Christ's idea of Christianity than that the triumph of the Gospel should be more dependent upon rich men than upon good men.

Are we not off the lines which Christ laid down? Give every man an opportunity of giving for his own sake, but not as if either God or the Gospel were in anywise his debtor. Make it a man's privilege to give; but, if it is other than that, realize that God will not accept it, and the church is better without it. We are off the lines. We have departed from this great fundamental truth of Christianity.

Instead of every Christian seeking and claiming the power from on high for the subduing of the world to Christ, we have come to think that Christianity means the safety of our own souls; and, as for everything else, it can be done by money. Actually, the church can never get money enough to do the work, and, that is the way God intends it to be. That is the first terrible mistake.

And the second grows out of the first, and aggravates it a thousand-fold. Since we look at Christianity as an arrangement for our own selfish security, the next step is to arrange for our selfish gratification in everything that has to do with it. Hugh sums of money may be lavished upon luxuries and elegance's which make the house of God the rich man's club, where a poor brother is an intruder. The Bible says in 1 John 3:16 "*We ought to lay down our lives for the brethren.*"

Do we dare to make the very worship of our crucified Redeemer that which ministers to our selfish comfort? Will Christ really bless this kind of expenditure? There is no command to give money to the church but that the church care for the poor is commanded again and again. This is made the very test and proof of our religion. We need the outspoken Apostle, James in our midst with his plain, strong words: "*My brethren, have not the faith of our Lord Jesus Christ, the Lord of Glory, with respect to him that weareth the gay clothing, and say unto him, sit thou here in a good place; and say to the poor, stand thou there, or sit here under my footstool; are ye not then partial in yourselves, and are become judges of evil thoughts? Hearken, my beloved brethren, hath not God chosen the poor of this world, rich in faith, and heirs of the kingdom which he hath promised to them that love him? But ye have despised the poor.*" (James 2:1-6).

No, it is not written anywhere in the scriptures that we must have money to be a good Christian. But it is written, "*Ye shall receive power after that the Holy Ghost is come upon you.*" (Acts 1:8). The fact is, that true Christianity is based on the principle of being wholly consecrated to Christ. If we try to work it any other way, we are beset and bewildered with failure. For this let us devoutly thank God. Only a holy church can ever be a conquering church. There is no other force that can reach the world with the gospel.

Chapter IV

OUR IDEA OF CHRISTIANITY: INTELLECTUAL POWER

Once more let us join the little company to whom has been entrusted this great work of restoring the world to Christ. Let us try to see the vastness and difficulty of the work as they must have seen it. There were rulers with their skill in crafty questions, the scoffing Sadducees and the Greeks with all their knowledge and subtle philosophies. Then there were the great nations north and south of them — Phoenicia and Egypt. It would certainly have occurred to us as the most natural thing in the world to say, "We shall need a great deal of intellectual power." In these clever times when everybody knows everything, and often is none the wise for it, there is a great need for us to realize that the Lord Jesus does not promise us intellectual power. He himself went forth from the midst of the people, and lived as one of the people. Those who sneer at uneducated preaching must beware lest their arrow strike him of whom it is recorded that "*the common people heard him gladly.*" (Mark 12:37). His power for preaching was the power of the Holy Ghost; and of all the purposes for which he received the baptism of the Spirit, this is placed first in order that the poor might have the gospel preached to them. His very method of preaching in parables was a miracle of simplicity; for anyone can understand stories like that of the Prodigal Son. While it is true that "*none ever spoke like this man.*" (John 7:46), yet it is also true that Jesus was a children's preacher. He chose to have about him plain men, who had no opportunity of study and no splendid gifts of intellect. His claim, as he stands in the midst of men and call them to himself, is that he is meek and lowly in heart; not on the grounds of great intellectual attainments, but as stooping to make great truths plain to the poor and needy, to the little and weak.

Later, when there came an apostle trained in all the learning of the Jew and the Greek, he, of all men, spoke most strongly against attempting to do the great work of Christianity by "*wisdom of words.*" (1 Corinthians 1:17). There is much need to listen to his warning: "*For Christ sent me not to baptize, but to preach the gospel, not with wisdom of words, lest the cross of Christ be made of none effect.*" (1 Corinthians 1:17). The divine authority which commissioned him to preach, equally forbade his preaching with wisdom of words. F. W. Robertson writes: "The wisdom of which Paul speaks appears to have been of two kinds of speculative philosophy and eloquence. The Greeks had deified wisdom, and Paul's language was that which ought to be written over the door of every school — We worship no Minerva, but Christ. It is important to dwell upon this, for there is in our day a marvelous idolatry of talent. It is strange and a grievous thing to see how men bow down before genius and success. Draw the distinction sharp and firm between these two things — goodness is one thing, talent another. The Son of man came, not as a scribe, but as a poor workingman. He was a teacher, but not a rabbi. When once the idolatry of talent enters the church then farewell to spirituality. When men look to teachers not for that which will make them more humble and God-like, but for the excitement of an intellectual banquet, then farewell to Christian progress."

These are strong words coming from one of the most gifted preachers of this age, but much stronger are the words of Paul: "*Christ sent me to preach the Gospel, not with wisdom of words, lest the cross of Christ should be made of none effect.*" (1 Corinthians 1:17). Preaching the gospel so cleverly as to undo and to destroy that which is preached, preaching the gospel, and yet only withering it and burying it! There is a well-known essay of Macaulay's in which he writes of the Puritans. "I have read it a score of times, yet scarcely once to think of the Puritans — they have always been lost in the brilliance with which they are described." The Cross of Christ is made of no effect! So must it be whenever a preacher or his people are turned aside from him by eloquence or philosophies about him. If the people go forth saying, "what a preacher!" instead of saying "what a Savior!" then is Christ hidden, and the cross of no effect through lack of wisdom. There are some good but mistaken persons who think dullness is piety, and that dreariness is sacred, their sign of grace is a groan, and they prove their religion by their misery. They estimate the worth of a sermon, not by its depth, or content, but by its length and, the great virtue of preaching is as an exercise in patience. All this is quite as far from the truth as is any "*wisdom of words.*"

Christianity invites and consecrates every gift of God, and every grace and art of which man is capable. There is room for money, room for enterprise, methods, learning, and genius. Nowhere can talent find so true and lofty an exercise, or indeed so sublime an inspiration, as in the service of Christ. If eloquence is gotten by burning conviction, where better to find masters of oratory where God has touched men's lips with his fire, to open people's eyes to see the realities of eternity and the infiniteness of God's love?

All gifts are good when they are used for the great purpose of the gospel; but, any gifts are perilous when the preacher or people are conscious of them. In a "sham" fight everybody admires the uniforms, the music, the horses, the precision of the march; but, in a real fight there is a desperate earnestness that cannot stay to admire anything that just girds itself up for death or victory. So it is in the church. If the gifts are used earnestly by Spirit-filled people who long to bring glory to Christ, then the more gifts the better. Without the Holy Spirit, gifts are a peril and a snare. When Christ says of men, "*Ye must be born again*" (John 3:3), what folly is it to go on playing with that which is utterly insufficient to accomplish the result, and then to wonder that nothing is accomplished! Nobody ever was or ever will be saved only through the preaching of the gospel. Preaching may indeed destroy the gospel. *"Ye shall receive power to preach after that the Holy Ghost is come upon you."* (Acts 1:8).   Until then our preaching is in vain. It is the gospel applied and enforced by the Holy Spirit which alone saves men.

Paul goes on at some length in 1 Corinthians. 1:18 to state the reason for his dread of all *"wisdom of words,"* and it is well for us carefully to consider this scripture. *"For the word of the cross is to them that perish foolishness"*. . . The very word *"cross"* meant both to Jew and Greek all that was most revolting. All that is associated with the word "gallows", and even more of indignity and shame, gathered about the word cross. There is no other word in any language that sums up so much that is offensive; a punishment of which Cicero tells us, that is so revolting that the very name ought never to come near the thoughts or eyes or ears of a Roman. And now, the Jews were to find their Messiah, and the Greeks were to discover the truth! Nothing could be more utterly hopeless, nothing more absurd. It is this very hopelessness of success, from a human standpoint, which shuts us up to the power of God. The cross is ever and must always be foolishness to men, except as they are enlightened by the Holy Spirit. To them it is the power of God unto salvation. *"For it is written, I will destroy the wisdom of the wise, and will bring to nothing the understanding of the prudent."* (1 Corinthians. 1:19). The reference seems to be to the invasion of Judah by Sennacherib, when Israel sought their safety in an alliance with Egypt. From a human standpoint it was a mark of their wisdom, but it was altogether contrary to the covenant and command of God. And their wisdom was destroyed by their being cut off from Egypt. It was a reed that could not support any, but which only pierced the hand that leaned on it. Not from Egypt, invariably a type of the world, but from heaven was to come their deliverance. What of this great host since the Lord was their Helper. How foolish, how useless their "wisdom." In the stillness of the night there went forth the angel of the Lord, noiseless, resistless; and when Israel arose in the morning, their dreaded foes were all "*dead corpses*" (2 Kings 19:35) as the record says. Full of meaning is the whole reference as if Paul would thus set forth the vastness of the work, the worthlessness of mere human wisdom, the power of God to save, and the complete triumph which is ours if we have him only as our strength. And then, as if he caught the gladness of those for whom such victory had been wrought, he cries, "*Where is the wise, where is the scribe, where is the disputer of this world? Hath not God made foolish the wisdom of this world?*" (1 Corinthians 1:20). Then the apostle goes on to inquire as to what wisdom had done in either knowing God or making him known. What had intellectualism achieved? The golden age of wisdom had come and gone. Homer had sung, Aristotle had taught, Demosthenes had spoken, and Socrates had lived and died; yet in Athens stood the altar to the Unknown God, and the restless world still looked vainly for the Savior. Now let the wisdom of the world stand aside and make room for foolishness of the Word, which is the power of God unto salvation.

"And look amongst yourselves," he seems to say, "those who have accepted the truth and are now to give it forth to others. There are not among us many wise, not many mighty, not many noble. God has chosen the foolish things of the world to confound the mighty." Human wisdom could not originate the gospel, human wisdom could not spread it at first, and human wisdom cannot sustain it now. Therefore, as it is written, "*He that glorieth, let him glory in the Lord.*"

"*So, then,*" he continues, "*When I came to you, I came not with excellency of speech, and this I did for a reason. I did not speak to you with enticing words of man's wisdom, but in demonstration of the Spirit of power, that your faith should not stand in the wisdom of men, but in the power of God.*" (1 Corinthians 2:5). That is everything. We can persuade men to agree with us, but what good is that? We can give them notions, theories, opinions, creeds, and these only mock them. "I see," men say, "but how can I be that which I see? Alas, the light is not the life. Power is lacking. Duties, ideals, dreams, may pass before me in surpassing loveliness, but what if I live just as far from my ideal as before?" What folly is our wisdom if these be only words. I want a mighty helper, an abiding presence, a transforming power. Here it is — "*that your faith should not stand in the wisdom of men, but in the power of God.*" (1 Corinthians 2:5).

I can tell a hungry man how many acres he can be lord of, how many buildings, how many servants, how many flocks, how many cars and how many luxuries he could want. And when I am done, will he go forth admiring the brilliant account of it all? What hungry man would not rather have enough money to buy a loaf of bread? Alas, it is only in religion that men play the fool thus, and are content with splendid notions.

Paul said, "*Howbeit we speak wisdom among them that are perfect.*" (1 Corinthians 2:6). What did the apostle mean? Perfect people want no wisdom. They are wise indeed, and no one can teach them anything. Here Paul gave us yet another reason against dependence upon wisdom in the great work of evangelism. Sin did not destroy in any wise our bodily organs, nor our mental perceptions; but, it did destroy the faculty of which Paul is speaking here — that spiritual sense by which we know God. We cannot see God with the eye, nor does our reason know God. We can perceive, perhaps, the need of some great first cause of things, but I do not know God in a logical way. How then do I know God? By a spiritual consciousness through which I commune with him, trust him, rest in his care, rejoice in his love, and set myself for his service; — a consciousness as distinct, as clear, and as reliable as any consciousness of my being. So then, when Paul refers to "*perfect,*" he is speaking to those who have had their faculties restored and to come with wisdom of words only would be to address the intellect. Whereas, to meet the need of the spirit, he must come with the power of the Spirit. "*As it is written, eye hath not seen, nor ear heard, neither have entered into the heart of man the things which God hath prepared for them that love him.*" (1 Corinthians 2:9). It is strange that this passage should have been so commonly supposed to refer to heaven. The apostle simply declares that the eye cannot see God, nor the ear hear him, nor can the natural man receive the things of God. "*But God hath revealed them unto us by his Spirit.*" (1 Corinthians 2:10). So then, because the realm of the things of God is spiritual and spiritual only, human wisdom is of itself incapable of either per-ceiving or receiving them; therefore, nothing can avail but the Holy Spirit of God. And as our knowledge of ourselves is only by the spirit that is in us, so the knowl-edge of God can only be made known by his Spirit which is given to us.

"The letter killeth." (2 Corinthians 3:6). With-out the power of the Holy Spirit, there is a deadening effect in the endless talking about Jesus, the familiarity with his name and story. How painfully sharp is the contrast between the sermon and the life. How real it is all outside, the streets, the people, the work, the wants of every day and hour; but, alas, how unreal is all that has to do with religion. Christ seems but a name, a memory, a solution for a problem, or a text for a ser-mon. How true it is — *"The letter killeth!*

But, the Spirit giveth life." (2 Corinthians 3:6). *"He shall testify for me."* (John 15:26); *"He shall glorify me."* (John 16:14). Then how real a presence is the Lord Jesus, the blessed brother whose very hand upholds us, whose love is our strength, and whose service is our joy, the one who comes to abide with us and commune with us.

That we might know the things which are freely given to us of God. That is the point at which our knowledge and God's revelation meet. All gifts are good that enable us to take possession of and to realize what God has given. Note the word — the things that are given — the things which God hath prepared and now spoken of as given.

Here is revealed to us very clearly the distinct work of the Holy Spirit — to put us in possession of all that God has given to us in Christ Jesus. God's love can never be greater, deeper, richer towards us than it is now — or, indeed, than it ever has been. His purpose concerning us can never be more glorious. Unasked, unsought, God has given us Christ, and, in giving us Christ, God has given us all that he ever can give. This is he by whom God made the worlds. Having given us Christ, the Father has said to us, "*All that I have is thine.*" (Luke 15:31). But the knowledge of what is given to us in Christ is to be opened up to us and put into our possession. And this is the work of the Holy Spirit — to glorify Christ, to make him our own as the realized gift of God. The heir to an estate may be but an infant of a day old, lying in his mother's arms, but the estate is his as legally and completely as it ever can be his. It is the knowledge of his possession that the years will reveal to him. This is the work which the Holy Spirit is come to do for us — that we may know the things of God.

That we might know the things that are freely given to us of God as it ever can be his. It is the knowledge of his possession that the years will reveal to him. "*He who knows the deep things of God is come to open up to us the fullness of which is ours in Christ.*" (1 Corinthians. 2:12b). This is the most pitiable thing under heaven — not that we are so poor, but that we are so rich, and do not know it. I once heard of a man who was worth three million dollars, he imagined himself a pauper, and lived on barely pennies a week and a loaf of bread.

What was he, pauper or millionaire? Both. He was actually a millionaire, but he thought himself a pauper. How sad. How many Christians are precisely that—

pauper millionaires, living on pennies and a loaf of bread, when all the unsearchable riches of Christ are theirs if they only realized it. We may know Christ on earth quite as much as we hope to know him in heaven. The Spirit is come to reveal Jesus as fitted exactly to all the common wants of our daily life and our earthly circumstances. He is to be patience for every worry, rest for our labors, and strength for every difficulty. The work of the Spirit, for which he has come to accomplish, is to reveal the Lord Jesus Christ exactly as we need to know him and to make us more than conquerors.

But this is not all. The gift of Christ is God's gift to the world. All about us are lonely, needy souls, knowing not of him who can heal their sorrows and sicknesses. Now our work comes in. Through us the Spirit is to reveal this gift, through us his love, his pity, his helpfulness are to be made known. In our lives his beauty is to be revealed. We are to go into the midst of men, and through us his truth and tenderness are to be set forth. For this we have been brought to the knowledge of his truth and faith in him, that through us the world around us may know the things that are freely given of God. For this work it is not logical skill that we need, nor great intellect, nor splendid gifts, but the wholehearted surrender of ourselves to this purpose, and the baptism of the Holy Spirit to accomplish it.

"*Ye shall receive power after that the Holy Ghost is come upon you, and ye shall be witness unto me.*" (Acts 1:9).

Chapter V

CHRIST'S IDEA OF
CHRISTIANITY: INDIVIDUALITY

Yes, Christ made room for all the disciples in all the variety of their character. There was no one chosen type to which they were to conform — "*shall be witnesses unto me.*" There was room for endless diversity of methods. There was no one system laid down which they were rigidly to follow. They began by speaking a dozen diverse tongues. The idea of Christianity is an individual consecration to Christ, for his glory and for the good of men, with room for every man's individuality.

Have not our rigid ecclesiastical and financial systems checked and even suppressed individual enterprise? Do we not need a great deal more generous freedom and opportunity for men to work for Christ in their own way? It is a very common thing for men and women of good position to go to all sorts of places — to

the heat of the tropics, to the perils of mountain climbing, to the winter of the Arctic regions in order to gratify
taste for travel, for research, or for pleasure, going at
their own expense, and putting up with all kinds of rude
discomforts. How is it that so very few, either men or
women, ever think of going without waiting to be sent,
or wanting to be paid, into the midst of such hardships
for Christ's sake? Yet with such a King as ours, and
with such a commission as that which he gives to all his
disciples, we should have looked for it to be a thing
most common. We should expect to see merchants re-
tiring at middle age from business in order to give themselves up to Christ's service. We should expect to see
men and women going down to live among their poorest and neediest brothers and sisters for the glory of the
Lord Jesus, who laid down his life for us. Is the love of
the Savior the only love that fails to kindle enthusiasm,
courage, endurance? Surely it should rouse the indignation of every man who loves God or who loves his
neighbor that an expenditure of money and trouble,
which is called self indulgence when it is to catch fish
or to hunt beasts for pleasure, should be called self sacrifice when it is to save men's lives. Do not let us doubt
for a moment that Christ will send us many such heroes as have been of old if only the church can make
room for them.

In science, the great discoveries have not been
made by appointment and direction of learned societ-
ies, but by an individual devotion to some one object,
by fresh and original experiments. A man makes a hobby
of his work, and surrenders everything to it — thought,
money, brain, heart — working away perhaps for years,

until the result is obtained. It is thus that great discoveries have been made and perfected, thus that great social problems have been solved, and it is thus that they have to be solved still. But unlike science with its welcome, the church has been terribly alarmed at individuality. New methods seem to suggest failure in the past, and that injures our pride. New methods smack of heresy, because they are new. There is in the churches a tendency to stateliness and dignity, which quenches the energy and enthusiasm of the Holy Spirit. Philip ran, and Peter took a beggar by the hand, and Jesus Christ took the part of a woman that was a sinner and healed her; but, such courses offend the refined tastes of a cultured and learned ecclesiasticism.

Is there anything sadder than the long list of prophets whom the church has first stoned and then erected splendid sepulchers to their memory? Foreign missions and Sunday schools were both denounced as full of peril. How pitiable is the history of the church in relation to the great questions of slavery, total abstinence, drugs and social purity. How pitiable that corruption and nonconformists over-rule. The churches today are unable to acknowledge a new idea, rejecting its validity until tested.

In business, great fortunes are not often made by old routines and ancient methods, but by men who can adapt, improve, extend — men who can manufacture a new article, or who go out to find a new market and who put daring, push, and resoluteness into their work. The great fortunes of the age have spent vast sums and great efforts to turn to account waste products. Now in the name of the Lord Jesus Christ, do let us encourage men and women everywhere to try their genius at saving the waste of humanity round about us — the waste of men and women and little children. Surely there is great need to find many new methods of successful service, and, for this work, be assured that God will give us men of genius and invention — only do not let the churches condemn them as heretics, or suspect them as fanatics. God does not waste his treasures, and may well with-hold such gifts if they are going to be frowned down by stately dignitaries who will not tolerate what they cannot control. We want more use of men and women in the ardor and flame of their first love to Jesus. We want to encourage men and women to try their own ways of doing good, without waiting for any authority except the prompting of their love to the Lord Jesus Christ, and the power of the Holy Spirit.

They all spoke with tongues, not as they heard other people speak, but as the Holy Ghost gave them utterance. They did not wait for any other permission, nor did they wait until they could speak with finished elocution or in proper sermonic form. To us, as much as to them, it is spoken — "*Ye shall receive power, after that the Holy Ghost is come upon you: and ye shall be witnesses unto me.*" (Acts 1:8). Do not let us think that this means great disorder, confusion, or lawlessness. Even if it did mean any such glorious confusion as they had on the day of Pentecost, let us not be frightened at that. Better that surely, a thousand times better, than the grim propriety of death. Let us be careful not to strangle any good man with red tape because he has his own methods. Do not put out the fire of God because it leaps and roars after its own fashion, instead of assuming a respectable size and pattern. *"Where the Spirit of the Lord is, there is liberty"* (2 Corinthians 3:17) — therefore give it room and opportunity. The church again and again lost much good wine because she would keep to her old bottles. The Episcopal Church lost John Wesley; and since then, had God sent us another Wesley, probably Methodism itself could scarcely have found him room. It is cheaper, and altogether better, to have, now and then, a new bottle, even though the shape be a little different and the capacity a little greater.

But, reader, what concerns you and me above all things else is this — that we do give ourselves with all our hearts to Christ. What great things can he do with any who is surrendered wholly to him — *"For the gifts and calling of God are without repentance."* (Romans 11:29). Therefore now, look up to him who looketh down upon you. Accept the call and claim which comes from him. Let yourself go — body, soul and spirit, to the great tides and currents of God's love that sweep about us. There is a music in the wind which has no voice until it reaches the tremulous and responsive wire — then it leaps forth in its power to thrill men. There is a meaning and a beauty and a glory in things, all unrevealed until they find the poet's soul — then they flash upon the world. There are a thousand forces in the earth, but they lie unknown until there comes some man of invention, by whom they are tamed and harnessed for service. The Christian is of higher rank than these, did he but know it. About us is an infinite love, and almighty power, and a yearning pity. Christ is what he is because he gathered this fullness unto himself, and poured it forth in human words of blessing, and stretched out hands through which its healing fell upon the people, and lived it day by day "*in perfect loveliness of deeds.*" Every man is a true Christian exactly to the degree in which this great love of God is turned to use and simple helpfulness. It is a wise and beautiful saying, "*He does the most for God's great world who does the best in his own little world.*" This is the meaning and purpose of our religion, that we should surrender every man his own little world to God, in everything for his good pleasure, that it be filled with his glory; to put him first in our thoughts, and in our desires, and in our ambitions; to measure life's greatness and joy by the opportunity it gives us for service to Christ. For this let us expect and claim the power of the Holy Spirit, that day by day, in all the round of life, we seek to bring in righteousness — rightness — which is the gold for the streets of the City of God; in everything to seek after purity of thought and purity of motive, which are as the crystal walls; and then in all to minister patience, and brotherliness, and love, which are as the balmy atmosphere of heaven.

Chapter VI

CHRIST'S IDEA OF CHRISTIANITY: THE PROMISED POWER

"Ye shall receive power, after that the Holy Ghost is come upon you." (Acts 1:8) — such was the promise. Now, it was precisely this element of power to subdue and possess the world which the religion of Jesus Christ seemed to lack; and, it was this power which the condition of these early disciples made most to be desired. The authority of Rome stretched on every side, haughty and triumphant. Her resistless legions were everywhere; her word was law; and little by little all that the Jew held most sacred was being lost.

This was quite as keenly felt by the Christians as by the Jews; for, the disciples of Jerusalem did not in any wise forsake the temple, or any of its rites of services, because they met together to break bread in the name of Jesus Christ. Now, in the presence of this invincible Rome, Christianity seemed but a poor defense compared with Judaism. So it came about that when the converts of Jerusalem were threatened with being cut off from Israel, their safety seemed to lie rather in giving up Christianity than in forsaking the religion of their fathers. Doubtless, they found in the religion of Jesus Christ a tenderness, a beauty, a compassion which they had not known before. But Judaism had in it a might and majesty which were much better fitted to cope with the evils about them. They admired the loveliness of Christ's character and his wonderful wisdom, and in happier circumstances it would be a joy to follow him; but a leader who bade them love their enemies, and who himself had died at their hands, did not give much promise of deliverance from the Roman power.

Let us remember, too, how very much easier it is for us to associate power with Christ than it was for them. For us, the blessed Lord is uplifted from our hard and common humanity; so that for us the difficulty is to realize his true brotherhood and oneness. Our thought of him is hallowed and beautified by all the most sacred associations of our lives; our imagination of him is shaped by the very masterpiece of art. But to them, that humanity stood out in all its coarse want and hardship, in all the surroundings of poverty and common toil. Here were men who had worked with him, who had journeyed at his side, wearied and dust stained as one of themselves. His kinsmen were with them, and talked of him as their own. Above all, they looked back to that life of lowliness through the death of the Cross; ever it stood out on the crest of the hill in all its naked shame and black dishonor. So, they thought of Jesus — a man born in poverty, often hungry and homeless, dependent upon the bounty of those about him; opposed by their rulers as an enemy to their nation; condemned by the priests as a blasphemer of their religion. They had followed him amidst the mob, and had seen him dying an accursed death. Now, while in this sorrow and death, love found its fullest claim and completest consecration, it is easy to see that in moments of doubt and fear these memories would come back to trouble the followers of Jesus. If their Master suffered thus, what hope was there for the disciple?

Now, from the lips of this same Christ, comes the promise — "*Ye shall receive power*" — power to subdue the world and restore it to him.

We have seen this power as it is set forth in the Gospels. It will also be interesting and profitable in every way to trace this power as it is set forth in the Epistles. We need the assurance of it today as much as the disciples needed it in their day. A greater belief in the power that is with us would cure the evils that grow out of our doubt and weakness. We live a long way below the idea of omnipotence. Our enterprises for Christ are by no means in keeping with our vast endowments. Our business is absurdly little compared with our capital. We measure our difficulties by human estimates only. We talk of temptations and trials as if we had to meet them all in our own strength. If we are of God, then is there only one motto, one boast, that is great enough to tell of our strength — "*I can do all things through Christ which strengtheneth me.*" (Philippians 4:13).

We will turn to the Epistle to the Hebrews, who, as the disciples of Jerusalem, were most exposed to peril, and who, therefore, needed most fully to know the power which is in Christ.

At the outset, the writer begins with that which was the very stronghold and refuge of the Jew — the ministry of the angels. The presence of the angels gave to their religion a heavenly loftiness, a stateliness, a majesty which seemed to be wanting in Christianity. The law was spoken of as received by *"the disposition of angels."* (Acts 7:53). The Jew thought of them as the sacred guardians of the very center and heart of his religion; the golden cherubim, with wings outstretched, hovered over the ark of the covenant. As in their perplexity and fear, Israel recalled the past, these watchful sentinels seemed to stand, excelling in strength, having charge over them to keep them in all their ways, and ever ready to smite in their defense. What glorious deliverances had been wrought again and again by the *"angel of the Lord."* In the bitterness of Egyptian bondage, the angel swept over the land, and in a single night the people were made free, and, laden with the spoils of their taskmasters, they marched out triumphantly to claim the land of promise. In times that were sad and troubled like these, when there was neither king nor prophet nor judge, the angel of the Lord led Gideon forth to victory, and had smitten the Midianites. An angel had told of Samson's birth, and directed his upbringing that he might destroy the Philistines. When the host of Assyria proudly demanded the surrender of Jerusalem, and defied the living God, an angel went forth in the darkness and smote the hosts. They re-

membered that Elisha was in Dothan, and the Syrian
king sent an army of men to take him, and they compassed the city until escape was impossible; then, at the
prophet's prayer, the young man's eyes were opened,
and lo, all round about him the mountain was full of
horses of fire and chariots of fire, and the enemy was
smitten with blindness.

What wonder, then, that at such a time as these,
threatened Hebrews should cling to a religion which
had such records of deliverance. When, besides these
treasured memories, there came that scene of Calvary,
where he hung without an angel to pity him or any to
deliver, little wonder that their hearts sank within them.
It is true that angels sang at his coming, and sat at his
tomb with glad tidings of the resurrection; but, they
wanted more than sweet hymns; they wanted the de-
stroying angel winging his way through the darkness,
breathing death upon Israel's foes.

Now, to meet this thought of the Hebrew, so
natural at such a time, the writer of the Epistle sets
forth the power of Christ as compared with the angels.
"You fear that as the disciples of Christ, you will lose
the ministry of the angels," he seems to say. No, indeed, in him only is their protecting service secured.
Jesus of Nazareth, the crucified and risen Lord, is infinitely more than they are. They wait upon him, listening to the voice of his word, and going forth at his bid-
ding to minister to them that are heirs of his salvation.
Then the writer turns to his own scriptures. Nothing
could be more masterly or sublime than the way in which
he exalts the Redeemer. "*To which of the angels said he
at any time, Thou art my Son, this day have I begotten*

thee?" (Psalm 2:7). A Psalm, full of the grandest poetry, it was only at a time of such peril that the stately music of its triumph could be fully appreciated. *"Why do the heathen rage, and the people imagine a vain thing? The kings of the earth set themselves, and the rulers take counsel together, against the Lord, and against his Anointed."* (Psalm 2:1,2). All untroubled, unmoved, there sitteth on the throne of the heavens the Eternal I AM, and turning to the Son he declares him to be the Eternal THOU ART. *"Thou art my Son, this day have I begotten thee."* (Psalm 2:7) Today, since his divine relationship could know no yesterday, no tomorrow. Where in the volume of the Bible is there any language like this spoken to the angels? They are but creatures, sinless and of vast intelligence, but forever separated from the Creator by an infinite distance. By a word that cannot be broken, to this Son is promised the heathen of his inheritance, and the uttermost parts of the earth for a possession.

Again, the writer turns to the great testimonies of the Scriptures, as he must speak the things which were written concerning the King. He takes them to the forty-fifth Psalm, which the Jews themselves applied to the Messiah, and which, indeed, it   is impossible to apply to any other. They must have seen again the Lord Jesus, and again have heard the gracious words which proceeded out of his mouth. *"Thou art fairer than the sons of men; grace is poured into thy lips: therefore God hath blessed thee for ever."* (Psalm 45:1,2). But this meek and lowly One is now the Captain of the Lord's host. *"Gird thy sword upon thy thigh, O most Mighty, with thy glory and thy majesty. And in thy majesty ride*

prosperously, because of truth, and meekness, and righteous-
ness; and thy right hand shall teach thee terrible things. Thine
arrows are sharp in the hearts of the King's enemies; whereby
the people fall under thee. Thy throne, O God, is for ever
and ever: the scepter of thy kingdom is a right scepter."
(Psalm 45:3-6).

This, then, is their Christ and ours; no more
only the poor and lowly brother of men, bone of their
bones, and flesh of their flesh, but seated upon the
throne of his glory, King of kings and Lord of lords.
What stability and assurance was theirs in him. In his
presence, what of the haughty Caesar; what of all the
forces of Rome? The scepter of righteousness which
sways the world is in the hand of the Crucified One.

Now comes the next step in the argument —
the way in which this Almighty Christ is going to subdue the world. That it is not to be accomplished by the
power of the angels, nor by the power of God outside
and apart from man. The power in which Christ went
forth to his work, the power which Christ promised to
the disciples, is the only power which can claim the
subjection of the earth.

Let us follow the argument. *"For unto the angels*
hath he not put in subjection the world to come." (Hebrews 2:5). The Greek word is the same as that used in
the fifth verse of the first chapter, and means the in-
habited world, the world of men. To whom then is this
world subject?

The writer goes on to quote from the eighth
Psalm, a Psalm of David. Across the plains, where the
flock lies in the dewy stillness of the night, we hear the
shepherd's hymn of adoration. *"O Lord our Lord, how*

excellent is thy name in all the earth!   Who hast set thy glory above the heavens. Out of the mouths of babes and sucklings hast thou ordained strength because of thine enemies, that thou mightist still the enemy and the avenger." (Psalm 8:1,2). Strange words, as if the psalmist looked and saw that deliverance and victory were to come, not by might nor power, but by the spirit of the Holy Child, by meekness and lowliness and trust. Certainly as we read we can only see Jesus.

Then David looked into the heights above him, where hung the hosts of silent stars; their calmness and purity seemed to shame the shallow, restless life. Thoughts of infinite space filled him; thoughts of the vast dominion which stretched on every side. Amidst these things how insignificant the span of human life — here today, tomorrow in the dust! "*Lord, what is man that THOU art mindful of him?*" (Psalm 8:4).

Yet this "considering" brought its own deliverance. For what were the bright worlds and all infinite space until man came to meditate upon them? The power to awe and to impress with vastness and duration was within him, and was greater than all these things about him. His lowly work as a shepherd testified to his kingship. Was not the world made for man, and did not all things wait until he came as rightful Lord to claim it? The earth was a wilderness until his toil made it a garden. The fruits were poor and scanty till his authority was felt by them. The plains were swamps or desserts until they came under his dominion and yielded their golden crops. The woods had no use, and the metals lay as idle ores, until he turned them to noble ends. The sea was a barrier of nations until he made it his highway. He sets the lawless winds to further his voyages or to grind his corn. The very stars themselves that seemed to be so much above him, man bade them be his great time pieces to measure the days and to mark off the seasons. Man is the appointed king.

Then, in the stillness of that night season, and with these meditations, came another thought which set upon him a crown of pure gold, and gave to him a glorious dominion indeed. *"Lord, what is man that THOU art mindful of him or the son of man, that THOU visitest him?"* (Psalm 8:4) God can visit man; and man can entertain his Maker. Within him are depths into which God can enter, a spirit with which God can commune, and, in this very possibility, is there not some dim yet awful indication and promise of the Incarnation, God manifest in the flesh? Was this the very purpose of man's being, the key to the mystery of his existence, that God should dwell in him, and that man, in who God should indeed abide, and through whom God should work perfectly, under him all things should be crowned with glory and honor?

Thus, then, the world waited for its king in such an ideal man. Certainly the king was not yet come. David was sometimes the slave, and not the king, the victim, and not the conqueror. The world waited for one who should render a perfect obedience, that he might claim a perfect dominion. When he came, we saw Jesus.

Now, he who has overcome the world by the power of the Holy Spirit says to us — *"Ye shall receive power, after that the Holy Ghost is come upon you."* (Acts 1:8). In that power we are to go forth, and to continue to complete the victory of Christ, until the kingdoms of the world become the kingdoms of our Lord and of his Christ.

This is Christ's idea of Christianity. It is not only a method for the pardon of our sins, it is not only a power by which we shall one day get to heaven, it is the power by which we are led into our true position as those who have dominion over the world to subdue it. The second Adam has regained for us our heritage, and now, by the might of indwelling God, we are to go forth and claim the world as his, and for him.

Let us see clearly of what this dominion over the "*world*" consists; for, the world is one of those which has had all the meaning beaten out of it, so that it has become little more than a sound. Man's original condition was not one of rest toward the world, but of infinite desire for God. There was a perfect contentment as to circumstances and man sought after God. But, with sin came the complete reversing of this order; and man's condition became one of unconcern and indifference toward God, while all the desire and longing of the heart went out after the world. Before the fall, man's natural gravitation was upward toward God, after the fall, it was downward toward the earth. Now it is this evil which Christ is come to undo. His very first sermon was a re-enthronement of man in his true position, freedom from anxiety and care for the world, that he might always and in everything "*seek ye first the kingdom of God, and his righteousness.*" (Matthew 6:33). Christ reveals to us the love and care of the Heavenly Father that he may put the world down and back in its right place. It was the promise of the victory, but the method was not yet revealed. It is by the indwelling power of God, the love of God shed abroad in the hearts by the Holy Spirit given unto us, that dominion over the world is ours. Care puts the man under the world, sets the world on top of his shoulders for him to carry; therefore saith Christ, "Be not careful." But when Christ reigns in the heart, then are we like Adam in paradise, the world is under our feet, and all the man is above it, with his affections set upon God.

So, then, do not run away from the world as if it were a foe that could not be fought. Do not abuse and condemn the world as if it were the devil's, it is the Lord's, and his is the fullness thereof. Now, our calling is to live so that through us the power of God may put the world in its right place. Let us go forth every day, with a whole-hearted surrender of ourselves to Christ for this end, and that through us he may subdue and claim and possess the world as his own. Thus, and thus only, shall he in the fullest and truest sense *"restore again the kingdom to Israel."* (Acts 1:6b).

Chapter VII

THE DISCIPLES BEFORE AND
AFTER PENTECOST

Paul prays for the Christian converts at Ephesus, that there may be given unto them *"the spirit of wisdom and revelation, the eyes of their hearts being opened, that they might know what is the hope of his calling, and what is the riches of glory of his inheritance in the saints."* (Ephesians 2:18). That he should give thanks for them, having heard of their faith in the Lord Jesus, and their love unto all the saints, is not strange; but, that he should then begin to pray for them and determine to pray without ceasing, may well appear strange. Had they not received the end of his prayers and their own when they found in Christ *"the gospel of their salvation,"* and when they *"were sealed with that Holy Spirit of promise."* (Ephesians 1:13). Now, relieved from anxiety on their account, the apostle may begin to think of others who are still unsaved. But rather now he seems to make these the special objects of his prayer. Our great anxiety is about those who are outside the church. Paul's anxiety is about those who are inside the church The reason lies very near the surface. A holy church means a conquered world and a glorified Savior; an unholy church is the only thing that can hinder the triumph of Christ. Therefore, having heard of their faith, he prays that God, the Father of glory, may give unto them the spirit of wisdom, that they may know what they have got in Jesus, and what Jesus has got in them.

So, then, this is evident, that we may have found in the Lord Jesus Christ "*the gospel of our salvation,*" that we may have been "*sealed with the Holy Spirit of promise.*" (Ephesians 1:13) or, in other words, what we have got in Jesus, and what Jesus has got in us. This knowledge is revealed to us by the gift of Pentecost. We may be true disciples and followers of Christ, and yet we may see in Jesus only what we want to see, and may never see at all what Jesus has in us. How this is made known to us in the Pentecostal gift is gloriously illustrated in the story of the disciples of old.

Let us begin this wonderful contrast at the incident recorded in the sixteenth chapter of the Gospel according to Matthew, where Jesus gathers his disciples about him in the quiet region of Cesarea Philippi. "*He asked his disciples, saying, whom do men say that I, the Son of man, am? And they said, some say that thou art John the Baptist: some, Elias; and others, Jeremias, or one of the prophets.*" (Matthew 16:13b). Well worth thinking of is that reply. This is the natural estimate of the Lord Jesus Christ, the world's opinion of him. Men set him as high as man had ever got, on a level with the greatest.

"He saith unto them, but whom say ye that I, the Son of man, am? And Simon Peter answered and said, Thou art the Christ, the Son of the living God." (Matthew 16:15,16). Not only alongside of the highest does Peter's faith set him, but higher than the highest could ever get; great not by attainment, but by origin, the Son of the living God.

In reply, the Lord Jesus tells Peter that it was not because of any special advantages that he had come to know this truth, not because he had seen what others had not seen, nor because he had heard what others did not know, he had no eye, no ear by which this could ever be learned. "Blessed art thou, Simon Bar-Jonah: for flesh and blood hath not revealed this unto thee, but my Father which is in heaven." (Matthew 16:17). So, then, here is a revelation of Jesus made to Peter by the Holy Spirit of God. "I say unto thee, thou art Peter, and upon this rock I will build my church; and the gates of hell shall not prevail against it." (Matthew 16:18). What the words meant it is not needful for us to consider just now; we are concerned with the meaning which the disciples would attach to the words. The Jew knew the church only as the kingdom, and the kingdom only as the church. Here, then, was that for which they so greatly longed, definite and assured; here was the promise of the triumph of Israel over the Roman power and other foes. This is what they wanted and longed to see. "And I will give unto thee the keys of the kingdom of heaven." (Matthew 16:19). The keys were the symbol of authority. All that Joseph was in the house of Pharaoh, Peter was going to be in the royal house of Christ the Lord. Now surely Peter's joy was full.

"*From that time forth began Jesus to shew unto his disciples, how that he must go unto Jerusalem, and suffer many things of the elders, and chief priests, and scribes, and be killed.*" (Matthew 16:21). As he bends over them, that face grows saddened, and he seems to say: "Come nearer to me, my children. I want you to see what you have got in me, and what I have got in you. I am come to suffer and to die. And now I want your tenderest love and sympathy and trust. I want you to comfort and help me with your heart's devotion. I am going to be killed."

Then Peter took hold of him, and said, "*This be far from thee, Lord;*" or, as it is in the margin, "*Pity thyself; this shall not be unto thee.*" (Matthew 16:22).

Jesus flung from his shoulder the too familiar touch, and said, "*Get thee behind me, Satan.*" (Matthew 16:23). Peter was doing the devil's work. What is that? It is one thing only — to make us think about ourselves.

Look at the the first temptation, when the devil came to our first parents, and with tones of indignant surprise began to inquire: "*So you are forbidden to eat of all the trees of the garden, such lofty and noble and sublime creatures as you. Ah, this is too bad. Think what belongs to you, the very top and crown of all things, ye shall be as gods!*" (Genesis 3:1-4).

Look at it in the case of the Lord Jesus: "*If thou be the Son of God, think of thy right, thy dignity, thy high position, and thy power, command that these stones be made bread.*" (Matthew 4:3). It is the devil's work still, "think of thyself." He cares little what we think of ourselves if we only keep on thinking it. Great saint or great sinner, it is all one if the eyes are set upon self. Mark well the one work of the Holy Spirit: to stay our thoughts upon God, to glorify Jesus, to set him before us, to reveal the love of God until our hearts cry, Abba Father. The one effort and life work of Jesus was to stay his mind upon the will of the Father, "*My meat and drink is to do the will of him that sent me.*" (John 4:34). So, then, Peter was doing the devil's work. "*Think of thyself.*" "*This be far from thee,*" "*this shall not be unto thee.*" (Matthew 16:22).

What follows? The beginning of the saddest chapter that was ever written in all the history of the church, the beginning of the dark sorrows of Jesus, not in the world, nor from his foes, but amongst his disciples. From that moment again and again we find Jesus alone. His thoughts are not their thoughts. They are eager for the temporal kingdom. His is conscious, day by day, of the shadow of the cross, ever nearer and darker.

There is a whole week of silence. It is as if time stood still, no word is spoken, no thing is done. O, that awful silence, in which no single word is recorded by the evangelists. How could there be anything to record? They would not hear of Christ's great sorrow, and so Christ could not have their love and sympathy.

A week of silence, and in his lonely grief the dreadful end shaping itself more vividly before him, until we can think that, unless some relief shall come, he must die. Three times in the life of the Lord Jesus it would seem that he, in all points like as we are, must have perished if help had not come from heaven. Once of bodily hunger, when earth had no hand to stretch out to the Lord of her harvests, and the angels came and ministered to him. Once of heart grief, when it would seem as if that heart must have broken as it broke on the cross, and there appeared an angel from heaven, strengthening him. This was the third time, when we can think that the human mind, burdened and crushed beneath such thoughts, must be overthrown unless he can find the relief which utterance and sympathy can bring. But, alas, even amongst his own disciples there is no ear, there is no heart. Then Christ goes up the Mount of Transfiguration. The angels could not help him now. They could bring him bread; they could afford him strength; but, of the mystery of the cross they could not speak. To them it was sealed, they desiring to look into these things.

There appeared Moses and Elias, talking with him of the decease that he should accomplish at Jerusalem. (Luke 9:30). Thank God that he had the two great saints of old waiting for that dreadful hour, that they with human sympathy could bring the Redeemer the relief which his own disciples withheld.

Look at it. Linger over it until it lives before the mind. Is it not the picture of the church today? We want the Christ that makes us happy, the Christ that is going to take us to heaven, and make us kings and priests to God, white robed and golden crowned. But in our midst today, there is a lonely Christ, carrying the sorrows of our poor world. He knows every perishing child, every outcast woman, every wretched drunkard and thief, every sad heart amidst the glitter of society and he comes to us to seek for our love, our sympathy, our service, that in us he may find his help. No, we do not want to know about these dreadful things. We want a nice, comfortable religion, which makes us forget all sorrow and wretchedness. Alas, the eyes of the heart are not opened. We cannot see what we have got in Jesus, and so we cannot see what Jesus has got in us. In Christ himself, indeed, we see not him so much as ourselves, we see only what we want to see.

The story grows sadder at every step of it. Henceforth, Jesus is alone, they will not hear, therefore they cannot help. Turn to the Gospel according to Mark, the ninth chapter and thirty-first verse. They have come down from the mount, and are passing through Galilee. And he taught his disciples, as if he said it over and over again, and put it many ways — *"The Son of man is delivered into the hands of men, and they shall kill him."* (Mark 9:31).

We see again that face so sorrowful, so full of entreaty; and, again he gathers his followers about himself, yearning for their trust and love. But they stood and stared with a heartless wonder, wishing that he would not talk of such dreadful things. They understood not the saying, and feared to ask him, lest they should understand.

"And when they were come into the house he asked them, What was it that ye disputed by the way?" (Mark 9:33). He had walked alone, or he would have known what they talked about. *"And there fell upon them all a silence and a shame. For by the way they had disputed among themselves who should be greatest."* (Mark 9:34). Think of it. Jesus alone burdened with dreadful thoughts of his own shame and agony and death, and on the breeze there came the noisy wrangling of his disciples

as to which of them should be the first. Alas, it is the picture still. The Christ alone, burdened with the sins and sorrows of the poor world; and, we behind him, every man eager for his own little gain, his own little position and dignity. Alas, who shall not pity him?

Turn to the tenth chapter of Mark, the twenty-eighth verse. *"Then Peter began to say unto him, Lo, we have left all, and followed thee."* (Mark 10:28). How foolish are we whenever we begin to boast, and how blind. This was the man who was hoping to be prime minister and lord of the treasury; and, this was he who was contending as to who should be greatest. Then, beside this boast, came words that are to be read very slowly, tarrying to let the vision rise before us. The figure of the Lord as he strides up the hillside, as if he had grit himself for some desperate purpose. The face was so white, so deeply lined with its sorrow. *"They were in the way going up to Jerusalem; and Jesus went before them,"* (Mark 10:32) — alone again, ever alone. As they followed they were afraid. Then he stops and leans as we can think, against the rugged trunk of some tree, and rests underneath the shade of its kindly branches. As the wondering disciples gather about him, surely it is with tearful eyes and lips that quiver in his grief that he begins to tell them what things should happen to him, that the Son of man was to be delivered unto the chief priests, and they should condemn him to death, and should deliver him to the Gentiles. With what terrible vividness does it stand out before him as he speaks? And he goes on to tell them how that the heathen should mock him, and should spit upon him, and should scourge him, and should kill him. Then, interrupting him in the very midst of these words, came one desiring to speak with him. The wretched wrangle has spread from the disciples to their family; and now comes the mother of James and John. Why, indeed, should Peter be first? He is not in the family. Geikie suggests that he was in an inferior position to the sons of Zebedee. It would seem, too, that there was a close relationship between Jesus and these two. So emboldened, the mother comes with her request, "*Grant that these my two sons may be sit, the one on thy right hand, and the other on the left, in thy kingdom.*" (Matthew 20:21).

So here, again, is the faith in Christ, believing in him, following him, yielding him its homage, yet the eyes of the heart are not opened, and therefore they see neither what they have in him nor what he has in them. So goes the burdened Christ alone, while his disciples are eager every one for his own position and greatness. So today the Christ is honored, adored, believed in, followed, but they who follow are seeking each his own happiness here and heaven hereafter and the great brother of all men, the helper of the needy, and the healer of earth's ills, can find no ear, no sympathy, no service, as he goes on his way.

But still sadder goes the story. Turn to the Gospel according to Luke, the twenty second chapter and nineteenth verse. The Master is sitting at the Last Supper. This very night begins that awful ending of it all and now he rises, and taking bread he broke it. Think how, in the act, the Lord passed through all the agony of the cross! "*Take eat; this is my body which is given for you.*" (Luke 22:19). So, for each the torn and broken bread. Then after supper he took the cup. How near,

how vivid, how real to him were all the sufferings of
that dreadful death as he spoke the words, *"My blood
which is shed for you."* (Luke 22:20). Then, there, right
under the very shadow of the cross there was a strife
among them, which of them should be accounted the
greatest.

Alas, it is our story, mine and yours. How often
in the very presence of Christ have we been eager for
our own importance, seeking through him to further
our little ambitions, so blind to his grief and so keen
eyed for ourselves, so dull to understand his will, so sen-
sitive to all that stirred our jealousy or pride. Let us
sink down in bitter shame at his feet. Is it always to be
thus? Christ bearing the sins and sorrows of the world,
and we going on in this dreadful selfishness? Is there
any remedy? If it is to be found, shall we not solemnly
resolve to find it? And if it is to be had, do we not
pledge ourselves that for our dear Master's sake it shall
be ours?

The day of Pentecost is fully come. The promised gift is given. Upon them has come the Holy Ghost,
and now they are witnesses unto him. The God of our
Lord Jesus Christ, the Father of Glory, has given unto
them the spirit of wisdom and revelation; and, now the
eyes of the heart are opened, and they see what they
have in Jesus and what Jesus has in them.

Perhaps, for the very first time, Peter ventures
to speak that dreadful word crucified. With what confidence he rings it forth. What a rapturous triumph it
kindles. What a tone of authority he catches as he
thinks of it. *"Ye men of Israel, hear these words; Jesus of
Nazareth, . . . whom ye have taken, and by wicked hands*

have crucified and slain: him hath God raised up." (Acts 2:22). What a victory this was, not only over-rulers and chief priests and Roman soldiers, but over death and all the powers of darkness. What a Christ this is, exalted far above the throne of David, to sit on the right hand of the Majesty on high, until his foes be made his footstool.

No more the poor earthly thought of a Christ who has come to indulge the selfish ambition of a disciple. Peter triumphed in a Prince and a Savior, who was exalted to give repentance and remission of sins. What has Jesus got in them? "*And they, continuing daily with one accord.*" One accord, all strife and wrangling dead. In that pure atmosphere envy and jealously can find no place, "*did eat their meat with gladness and singleness of heart;*" (Acts 2:46), as if one great brotherly spirit dwelt within them. "*They had all things common,*" (Acts 2:44), how complete and perfect the transformation. "*They sold their possessions, and parted them as every man had need.*" (Acts 2:45). The glorious change fills every page, gleaming, flashing everywhere.

Peter and John went up together. Together, that is a new thing. Were they not the rival claimants of all opponents first and strongest? But now there is no separating them. Here is some acquaintance of Peter's who stops him for a moment. "Excuse me, Peter, but a little time since, when I met you, things were looking very bright. You expected to come into a position of vast influence and wealth — prime minister, keeper of the keys of the House of David.. May I ask after your position? I see you have come into a fortune, you look so happy."

"*Silver and gold have I none,*" (Acts 3:6), cries Peter, but without a hint of disappointment or regret, he does not seem to think about it for a moment. See what Jesus has got in Peter, one who cannot pass a beggar without pity and a great longing to help him. See what Peter has got in Jesus Christ, not one who is going to make him rich and happy and great, but one who through him can bend over a lame man and lift him up and set him on his feet.

"*Peter took him by the right hand . . .*" (Acts 3:7), took the beggar! Really, Peter, great apostle and bishop, trusted with such awful authority, first of a line of wondrous successors of lords, spiritual and temporal, who in their splendid pomp shall claim to be the keeper of thy keys, be not so forgetful of thy dignity and high position as to go taking beggars by the hand. Ah, Peter has forgotten all about himself. The love, the pity, the mighty helpfulness of Jesus Christ fill all his soul. "*In the name of Jesus Christ of Nazareth, rise up and walk.*" (Acts 3:6b). And Peter watches the man going, leaping, and praising God; he knows more joy and blessedness than ever came to prime minister or lord of the treasury.

Follow the story. Things get worse and worse for Peter. Poor Peter, how disappointed he must be. The last time we saw him he had neither silver nor gold, and now they have taken him off to prison, and tomorrow he is to be brought before the judges. Or, follow them as they go to their own company, and join in that praise meeting. What a might as of omnipotence these men find in the very name of Jesus. What a defiance of triumph. What a great untroubled rest is theirs as they sing of him, and of the signs and wonders that shall be wrought in the name of the Holy Child Jesus!

Worse yet, poverty was bad, prison was worse, but now, here come the apostles, beaten, bruised, bleeding, their dreams of greatness have had a rude awakening. What now of their strifes and ambitions?

Beaten, what indignity and shame is this? But follow them. "*And they departed from the presence of the council, rejoicing that they were counted worthy to suffer shame for his name.*" (Acts 5:41)

What do you think of a Christianity like this? It is ours, yours and mine, if we will have it. Doesn't it kindle our longing, and don't our hearts cry out for so complete a surrender of ourselves to Christ? Claim the promise, for it is yours. "*Ye shall receive power, after that the Holy Ghost is come upon you: and ye shall be witnesses unto me.*" (Acts 1:8).

Chapter VIII

THE POWER COMES: THE DISCIPLES AMONGST THE ROMANS

The day of Pentecost is fully come. The disciples are filled with the Holy Ghost, and now they all go forth to be witnesses unto Christ. Do not for a moment think of them all as preachers, and not even of all as doing any distinct and definite work in the church. But all alike go forth to be witnesses unto him, to live over again the life of the Lord Jesus Christ. For this, above everything else, is the power given. They might preach, but the preaching was an empty word without the Christ-like life. The world was to be won, not by theories, creeds, methods, but by Christ-like living. Men and women were to go in and out amongst their neighbors, doing their daily work, giving their evidence for Jesus by living him, their lives examined and cross examined, but their testimony holding good. Whatever difference could it make to anybody that any man should say that Christ was the Son of God, and that he rose from the dead, and that he had sent them out in his name to claim the world for him? The world might well laugh them to scorn, "What do these feeble Jews think they can do for him?" But when each of them went out to live a Christ-like life, it made a vast difference to everybody — a life of truth, of purity, of self forgetfulness, of helping everybody, of loving everybody — a life loosed from the pleasure and pride of the world, from the tyranny of its maxims and spirit; a life lifted up from the littleness of the seen and the narrowness of the present, laid out in relation to the eternal and the infinite. Men could not help feeling that and believing in it. Very likely, they hated the light that condemned them, the goodness that shamed them, but they could not be indifferent to it. Their very persecution was aimed against its power; it was the acknowledgment, *"This is the heir; come, let us kill him, that the inheritance may be ours."* (Matthew 21:38). Better, a thousand times better, a persecuted Christianity than a religion which is too weak or too worldly to make anybody feel uncomfortable. Christianity is Christ-likeness, that or nothing.

So, then, the little company, carrying its sacred trust, goes forth into the midst of the great world, simple goodness against the combined forces of the earth. Which shall win, shame, indeed, to any with whom the answer is a doubtful one? The answer is triumphantly assured, that shall win which has God on its side. Would to God that his people only believed it.

Let us follow them as they come into contact with the Roman — stern, haughty, commanding a nation that worshipped authority, whose system of military organization was more complete than anything the world has seen, before or since. At the very dawn of Christ's day, we see this power of goodness face to face with the might of Rome. In his strong fortress, amidst his lords and chief captains and his men of war, is the proud Herod, representative of Rome. And before him comes the last of Jewish prophets, the first of Christian preachers — John the Baptist, friendless, helpless, not knowing how long he may call his head his own. Could any contrast be greater, Herod, in his royal apparel, with power of life and death upon his lips; and, this pale faced prisoner, his home the dungeon, the fetters on his wrists? But as John speaks a few plain, strong words, Herod cringed — the soul sank within him, and amidst his men of valor, with Rome at his back, he felt that all his forces, and all Caesar's legions were no match of this prisoner. Herod feared John, knowing that he was a just man and a holy. Look at it again in the person of the blessed Lord Jesus before Pontius Pilate, the Roman governor. O, never was one so helpless as he was at that hour. Wasted and wearied, see him as he is grasped by the rough soldiers, beaten, bound, forsaken, with all the marks of his foul dishonor about him. They have plucked the hair of his cheek, they have scourged him, and spit upon him, and buffeted him. On every side of him is the surging mob. Now Pilate comes, scornful of these Jews and their superstitions. With a tone of derision he asks, *"What accusation bring ye against this Man?"* (John 18:19). Yet, in this man there is something that strangely moves Pilate, a dignity, a depth of pity, the patience as of God.

He has heard the charge against him, and now beckons the soldiers to bring him within the hall. There Pilate looks into that face, so infinitely sad, and yet so unearthly in its majesty and love. *"Art thou a King?"* (John 18:33), he asks, a question that could only be put to such an one in derision or in awe. It is with awe that Pilate goes forth and cries to the accusers, *"I find no fault in him."* (John 18:38b). Later we read: *"he (Pilot) was the more afraid."* (John 19:8). Afraid! So friendless, so powerless, so completely in the hands of Pilate, surely thou dost not fear him! Then was Pilate the more afraid when he heard that he made himself the Son of God. (John 19:7). The might of that simple goodness was more than a match for all Rome, and the Galilean conquered. And one can think that it was with the confession of his heart that Pilate wrote: *"This is the King of the Jews."* (John 19:19).

Look at it again, as Paul stands before the cruel Nero — Paul, the aged, Paul who writes that none stood by him. What of the threats of the emperor, "I will cut off thine head?" Think how Paul's face lights up with gladness, and, looking heavenwards, he cries, *"Henceforth there is laid up for me a crown that the Lord, the righteous Judge, shall give me in that day!"* (2 Timothy 4:8). What could they do with such a man? To kill him was only to insure his coronation. The arm of Rome was paralyzed, she had no hand that could injure him. This was the power that smote Rome — the conquering power of simple goodness, the goodness of God, of Christ, lived out in the power of the Holy Spirit by plain men and women.

This is the want of today as of all time. Give us this goodness, and the victory is assured. Nothing else will avail us anything. We have a foe to fight in our land today, mightier than ever was in Rome of old. What is the great power of the state, the God of this country, enthroned and crowned, and served with an intenser and keener and more exacting service than ever slave or soldier rendered to the emperor of old?

Gold, the thirst for it, cruel and terrible, sometimes as the thirst of hell, the means of making it, and knowing no law but success, that sanctifies everything, the ways of spending it or not spending it, these three are the sources of the ills that curse us. All this Christianity scarcely touches, how is it? Its voice is scarcely lifted against this haste to be rich, to get on in the world, no matter who is driven to the wall. Has Christianity a message? Has it any remedy for this state of things, this growing poverty of the poor, this growing wealth of the wealthy, and between them a gulf ever deeper and broader, with its awful squalor and wretchedness on one side, and its splendid luxury on the other? Is the Christianity of Christ, which was able to conquer the Caesars, able to meet these evils? If it can, then in the name of our God, let it be used, for there is terrible need. Does somebody object that such Christianity is revolutionary, that it is Socialism? Well, let us ask ourselves the plain truth about these dreadful words. Is Christianity a conflict with evil only amongst the poor, the weak, those who have little choice between vice and starvation? But if evil be rich, and wears a crown and sits on a throne, is Christianity to bow down before it, and call it law and order? Let no man pretend that the Chris-

tianity of Jesus Christ is that. His Christianity is in conflict with evil everywhere. Within a week of Pentecost
the leaders of Christianity were in prison, and refused
to give any promise to the authorities that they would
recognize any law which was contrary to the command-
ment of God. Paul and Silas did not intend to interfere
very seriously with some rich men's gains, and go beaten
for it and sent to prison, and they praised God when
they got there.

Men seem utterly to forget the warnings of God
against this feverish rush and haste to be rich. If thought
of at all, they are considered to be the wild and somewhat mistaken words of men in an age when they "did
not understand business." It is almost impossible for
the Gospel voice to make itself heard in this matter,
amidst the din and hubbub of life. It is difficult to reach
the cities, there is too much vibration, and the skies are
too stained with smoke. Alas, there are heavenly signs
and warnings and entreaties which the church fails to
hear, is too busy, perhaps too greedy. There is the gospel of contentment, the gospel which Christ preached
in his first sermon, and in the whole sermon of life. "*Ye
cannot serve God and Mammon;*" (Luke 16:13; Matt.
6:24); therefore, let the anxiety for Mammon go that
ye may serve God.

Who of the hurried, anxious, eager ones that
fill our streets and market places really believes that?
How utterly lost and dead, tramples under foot on the
hard pavements of our cities, are such sweet messages
as these which God hath sent to us — "*Be ye free from
the love of money; content with such things as ye have: for
himself hath said, I will in no wise fail thee, neither will I in*

any wise forsake thee." (Hebrews 13:5). Never were words more true, Paul felt, men greedy for gain would not hear — Godliness with contentment is great gain. "*For we brought nothing into the world, and it is certain we can carry nothing out. And having food and raiment, let us be therewith content.*" (1 Timothy 6:7).   That is the gospel of Jesus Christ, in the very teeth of the man-made gospel of this century, the gospel of push, of getting on in the world. Then, from this clear sky comes the thunderbolt, as if there were no choice between this divine contentment and this peril.: "*They that will be rich fall into temptation and a snare, and into many foolish and hurtful lusts, which drown men in destruction and perdition. For the love of money is the root of all kinds of evil: which some reaching after have erred from the faith, and have pierced themselves through with many sorrows. But thou, O man of God, flee these things.*" (1 Timothy 6:9-11).

Reader, put it to thine own heart: Is God and his service more than the world? Is the uncertain gain, which I must leave behind me, more than the abiding character which I must take with me forever? Is Christ the King more than Mammon? Is not anything better that the feverish unrest and disquiet and burden of care, if only it gives us opportunity and desire for communion with God, and growth importance, and in the earthly security and independence which come with wealth?

For this, the power of the Holy Spirit is given, to cast out the devil of covetousness and love of money, and to bring into the life a gracious contentment. Was there ever more need to seek that power, and to wait upon God until it is given? The promise is yours. What will you do with it?

This gospel of contentment would go very far to remedy the second great evil, "the method of making money." The Christianity of Jesus Christ is a power in the midst of us to cast out of business the keen, hard, advantage taking spirit that finds its opportunity in other men's difficulties. "If I did not, somebody else would." Very well, let somebody else do it; but, for Christ's sake, you dare not do what is unbrotherly. What others do is surely no law to a man who calls Jesus Christ his Lord and Master. We have no business to trust him as our Savior if we do not follow him as our example in every path of our life. The religion of Jesus Christ forbids utterly the underhandedness or misrepresentation that the world calls clever. It forbids the many words of bargaining, and denounces utterly the whole system of bribes and thefts. Now, it is sheer and utter folly; it is worse, it is a miserable and dreadful hypocrisy, for any who do these things to profess and call themselves Christians. Christ never knew such Christians, and will not own them.

Some years ago, I heard of an honest man who occupied a position of great responsibility and influence as manager of a large company. A merchant called upon him one day, anxious to sell some steel, and quietly set down before him a roll of money. "What is this?" asked the manager. "O," explained the merchant, in an undertone, "If you will be good enough to accept it with the compliments of the firm." Then it flashed upon the good man that it was a bribe. Crumpling the money together as so much waste paper, he flung the bills out of the office door, and said indignantly, "Sir, if you are not gone after them in one minute, I will kick you there!"

That is the Christianity for this century, that resoluteness in the soul, in the hand, yes, and in the foot too, if need be. The Christianity of Jesus Christ is a power stronger than the power of money.

What is the good of all our churches and chapels, our sermons and services, our preachings and prayings, if we cannot find in them all a power that can make honest men? What is the gospel of Jesus Christ for if it is not a power to make men speak the truth exactly, whether it pays or whether it does not pay? If we cannot find in Christianity a power that can secure that, then let us have done with it. Turn the churches and chapels into hospitals, to some other purpose, and send all ministers at least to earn an honest living. The Christianity of Jesus Christ is a power to make men honest, true, upright, and to keep them so, or it is nothing, and worse than nothing.

Does somebody suggest that you cannot do business on those principles? So it has been said. Very well, if that be so, what then? There was a time when men could not be Christians and live; so they were Christians still — and died. If it comes to that, there is no good reason why we should not go and do likewise. At least be one thing or the other. If you want the world, choose it and make the most of it, but do not call yourself a Christian. If Christ be King, and you profess to be his servant and soldier, then be true to him. *"No man can serve two masters... Ye cannot serve God and Mammon."* (Matthew 6:24). Christ is the King.

He must reign. Will you bow before him now, reader?
Will you, in his strength, gird yourself afresh for his service; kneel at his feet, and pledge yourself to be true
and faithful to him, his brave soldier at all times, and in
all places, and in all companies, and amidst all perils,
carrying this awful trust — the glory of the Lord?

Chapter IX

THE DISCIPLES AMONGST THE GREEKS

Let us follow the disciples again — these men and women filled with the Holy Spirit, and going forth to be witnesses to Christ. We have seen them coming into contact with Rome, in the might of their goodness subduing the force of her legions. Now let us follow the effect of the Christ-like life amongst the Greeks. Once more let us guard against thinking of these early disciples as preachers. Our notion of them is apt to be shaped by the recollection of Peter in Jerusalem, or Paul on Mars Hill, or Appollos. The disciples then, like the disciples today, were simple men and women, for the most part of the humblest position, many of them probably slaves.

Now, what can these do amongst a people like the Greeks — a nation of philosophers, intellectual, of most fastidious taste, looking with the utmost contempt upon the uncultured and ignorant? What chance had a handful of despised Christians of influencing such a people? It seems a more hopeless task than their work amongst the Romans; for their rough strength would more easily be wrought upon gentleness and love than these refined Greeks would be influenced by those whom they so ridiculed and despised. If ever intellectual power seemed a necessity, it was here. Many a lowly follower of Christ must have sighed, "O, that God would send us some genius that should confound the reasonings and overthrow the philosophies of these mighty men, and show that Jesus is indeed the Christ! Would God that I were clever." And the lowly one sighed again to think how little good he could do. It was all right. The only power needed was the power given; power to live over again the Christ-like life — that was the supreme argument. "But this Christian disciple is a slave — of all most ignorant; one whose opinion nobody would ever consider worth hearing. Have you any hope of men in his position transforming the customs and systems of these cultured and elegant Greeks?" So I can think of some early Mr. Fearing talking of their needs. "Nothing will be done here without orators, men of splendid gifts and genius, they are needed for this work." Does not He who ascended up on high, and received gifts for men, know the gifts that are required? Alas, that we are so much more ready to suggest than to receive.

Let us stay awhile here amidst those who are waited on by this Christian slave. Here is the master of the house, a doctor in philosophy. With massive head and brows knit in earnest thought, he dreams his dream.

"I can think," he mutters to himself, "if there should come from some other world — if indeed there be another world" (for the sign of a true philosophy is that same if, to be sure of anything is unphilosophical) — "one of the gods, if gods there be; in the likeness of us men — if indeed there be any men; I can think that, should such an one gather about him a company of disciples, and then, for the sake of the truth he taught, should lay down his life, that the memory of such a leader, treasured and obeyed, might perhaps come to inspire a purely unselfish life." As he dreams his dream, his slave is busied about a thousand things in the house, moving ever to and for, in his gladness singing some song of his Redeemer. Some day the philosopher wakes up, and rubs his eyes, and watches, as one whose suspicion is aroused. He tests this slave, and watches more narrowly, and from every test he comes triumphantly. The master can resist it no longer. "He has got it," he cries; "This slave of mine is living the life. He tells of One who has indeed come down in the likeness of men, and who has laid down his life for the truth he taught; and he claims that not the memory only, but the very presence and power of this same crucified one controls his whole life, and shapes his every wish and word and act." Ah, poor slave, give thanks to God. No orator, no philosopher, could do so much, no genius could do so well. Amidst the splendid visions of these men, the unselfish dreams and the selfish lives, here was a bit of actual flesh and blood translating the vision into everyday life. That is Christianity — earth's sublimest aspirations, most splendid visions, loveliest dreams, embodied and lived, yet without any least consciousness of sublimity or loveliness. The Christ-like life is the only power that can subdue the world.

Recall, again, the restlessness of the nation, the uncertainty about everything. Here and there was a man, a woman, whose life seemed all sunshine, peace, repose. A people so full of perception could not fail to detect it in the look, the tone, the manner — everything. The only explanation was that these knew of One whom they called Father, whose faithfulness was a rock upon which they built for eternity, whose love compassed them as heaven compassed earth.

Their lives were blessed and bright with hopes which, like the flowers, had their roots in the earth, but that stretched up into the sunshine and favor of God.

Think of the nation, again, in its search for happiness, toiling for rest, lavishing money upon pleasures that ceased to please, and greedy for luxuries that only burdened them more. Amidst the sculptured marbles and splash of fountain, and the charms of exquisite beauty, here leans the fair Greek. From the terrace below there comes the voice of the slave telling of one who wrote from his prison, "*I have learned, in whatsoever state I am, therewith to be content.*" (Philippians 4"11).

Some day, half scornfully, and yet with whole-hearted longing, the Grecian lady asks, "Tell me, what is this silly nonsense that you have in your head that you call your religion?" O happy disciple, with such an opportunity. As the eye flashes and the face lights up, the heart pours forth its story of God's love and of the Blessed Christ; that we are not the sport of lawless chance, but that we are guided by infinite wisdom, we are led by his hand, that all life is not a vexation, a weariness, a fear, but an education, a development, a gracious unfolding, like the unfolding of the lily at the touch of the light and warmth; and, that God has one great purpose running through all things, shaping them, through pleasure and through pain, through loss and gain, through health and sickness and through death, that we be conformed to the image of the Altogether Lovely, and that all within us be made beautiful as God.

Here, truly, was a philosophy not dreamed of only, but possessed; not argued about, but lived. It was the power of that life of rest, of sweet unselfishness, of trustful happiness, that won the Greek for Christ. Alas, that any should go sighing for thoughts and words to tell of it when they can have that very life itself, and be like Christ.

We live today in a very revival of the Greek spirit. Art, philosophy, music, culture, have asserted their power as never before. We are conscious of it every-where — in our buildings, in the very shapes of things, in the restless skepticism of the age. The pulpit, the press, the whole literature of the land testify to its sway. There are the same characteristics in the people as in the Greeks of old — the restlessness, the intellectual-ism, the craving for excitement, the weariness, and the skepticism. How are we going to meet it? There is but one thing needful — that those who are called Chris-tians will set themselves for Christ's sake to live the Christ-like life, striving to let men see in everything the truth and purity and courageous goodness of Jesus Christ — his graciousness and lowliness, his patience, and yet his indignation, too, against all evil — striving to bring into the world the hope for all men, and the help for all which comes from faith in God and his self-sacrifice. We have no right to sigh and think how difficult it is to live such a life. If Christ offers us the power, where is the difficulty, except only that we do not accept it? This Christ-like life alone is Christianity. Do not let us think of it as anything less or anything else; and it is power for such a life that is provided for each of us.

This alone will suffice. Books on the evidences of Christianity may interest as arguments; may even silence some objections, unless they provoke further controversy. The power of the Holy Spirit is not an intellectual power to prove the abstract truth of Christianity; it is a power to let men see and feel the living Christ. There is only one work on the evidences of Christianity that wholly satisfies any one, a work which defies the most ingenious criticism and the most skillful logic. It is said to be scarce, if not indeed very scarce, but we have met with it here and there. It is from five to six feet of humanity living a Christ-like life.

What is it that keeps religion alive in our land today? What is it that creates and sustains faith in God and in the unseen, and in the reality of a power that can make men what they should be? It is the Christ-like life. In the school, some one boy setting himself to be a faithful disciple of Jesus Christ. In the office, or the workshop, or the home, one resolutely following in the footsteps of Christ. In the market, one whose word is ever true, whose dealing is ever honorable, whose integrity and uprightness never fail under any strain. These are the props and pillars of Christ's religion in our land today. Intellectual power, social position, money, these do count for very little. Here is a man occupying a high position in society, refined, keeping himself abreast of the thinking of the age. He has been reading some article either for or against Christianity; has been somewhat interested in the argument, and now puts down the book probably to forget all about it. And now he rides to church, for it is Sunday morning. He has heard scores of sermons, but probably cannot recall one of them. Now as he rides through the village street, here is old Hodge. I know him well, poor old fellow, bent and dried up in the winds and sunshine of seventy years' hard toil.

"Good morning, Hodge," says the squire, reining in his horse.

The old man lifts the trembling hand to the rim of his battered hat. "Good morning, your honor, good morning," and the face beams with gladness.

As the squire rides slowly away, listen, for it is worth hearing. "Poor old Hodge, if ever there was a good man under the sun that is old Hodge. I would give half my acres if only I had got in my heart what he has got in his."

Look at him again, poor old Hodge — intellectual power? — No, he does not know his A,B,C's. Money? — His income is two shillings and sixpence a week, and a loaf of bread. Social position? — Next Saturday he is going into the almshouse.

O, is it not a glorious thing that this holy religion of Jesus Christ is a thing so sublimely indifferent to all these earthly considerations. Give her goodness, goodness only, unfailing Christ-like goodness, and her victory is assured. Nobody stops to ask what denomination that belongs to, or what distinctive creed it may hold. The heart cries out, "That is what I believe in, and that is what I want to be." Whatever else men do believe in or do not, everybody believes in goodness. That needs no other words to claim it. Like the sun, its voice is not heard; it is enough that it shines.

Chapter X

THE DISCIPLES AMONGST
THE POOR

Once more let us follow these men and women filled with the Holy Spirit as they go amongst the poor, the outcast and enslaved. There were plenty of these in the days of the early Christians. These great masses of the poor and destitute are not of the creation of modern life.

It is the question that every Christian should ask himself — Has Christianity any message, any remedy for the social ills of our time? If it has such a message, what is it? There is a perilous seething in our midst. It is as if our great cities were built over slumbering volcanoes, and ominous disturbances now and then remind us that the internal fires may easily break forth and overwhelm us. Yet the Christianity of today seems for the most part to go on its way wrapt in its self complacency, and not greatly concerned about anything beyond trying to make its fortune, and then to find its own way to heaven. Verestchagin, the Russian painter, soldier, and traveler, whose observation and experience give weight to his words, makes this statement in his autobiography: "We shall search in vain for Christian communities where the precepts of Christ are really carried out."

What then of the early Christians filled with the Holy Ghost in relation to the poor? Well, they did not wait until they had some particular remedy, defined and approved, for this particular ill. They never dreamed that they were going to introduce a revolution. They had two things, the only two things that Christianity requires. They had the example of Jesus Christ, and they had power to follow his steps. That wrought the revolution, just as when God turns the dead world of winter into the beauty of spring, by the warmth of a new life, a life of love.

Let us, too, carefully look at the example and teaching of Jesus Christ in relation to the poor. By his very coming, Christ made poverty no more a degradation. Of all men who ever lived, Jesus Christ alone had choice in the circumstances of his birth, and he chose the poorest lot and the hardest fare that ever befell any man.

Henceforth, poverty was no part of divine disfavor. He who became poor was the well loved Son in whom the Father was ever well pleased. We cannot measure God's goodness by income.

Jesus Christ took away the reproach of poverty. But, alas, the great example does not affect men's estimate of poverty today. Jesus Christ lowered the great-

ness of wealth by passing it by, and uplifted and hallowed the life of poverty by deliberately accepting it.
But more than this, much more; the one supreme idea
which Jesus Christ lived out to the full was this, a true
brotherliness. For the first time in all the ages, Jesus
Christ brought into the world a reverence for humanity. Everything in His life, lights up his brotherly kindness. His deeds, his words, his manner, his look, his
death all grew out of it; his gracious familiarity, his simplicity, his perfect approachableness and homeliness —
all proclaimed it. If so varied and many-sided a life can
be put into a single word, this the the summary of its
earthward aspect — it was perfected brotherly kindness. This inspired his teaching and his actions, and
his fiercest indignation was kindled by all that made
light of this great law of love. His parables, alike in
their sweetest tenderness and their most lurid terror,
set it forth again and again. His revelation of the Father established a new relationship amongst men; now,
all were brought nearer to one another, and now they
are brothers. The very word humanity and the idea
which it expresses came in with Christ, never before
had the oneness of the human race been thought of. It
is this sacredness of human nature, its greatness, its dignity, which is declared and secured by the mystery of
the Incarnation, that God should dwell in man; by the
crucifixion, that for man he should lay down his life; by
the resurrection, that man should be exalted above all
principalities and powers, and should sit upon the throne
of heaven beside the Majesty on high. This reverence
for humanity constantly meets us in the utterances of
Jesus Christ. He asks, *"What shall it profit a man, if he*

gain the whole world, and lose his own soul?" (Mark 8:36).
Though the man be filled with vice, though he be too
bad for earth and fit only to be nailed to the cross, yet
so dear to Christ that such an one is reckoned worth
dying for.

Now his followers go forth into a world redeemed, not with silver and gold, but with the pre-
cious blood of Christ. Men were made in the image of
God, women were held in great love, and little children were sacred and blessed by His hand. Of theories, theologies, definitions, these disciples perhaps knew
very little; but, love is truest knowledge, and love to
everybody was supreme.

What a great outburst of brotherly love fills the
early chapters of the Acts. He who was rich and for
their sakes became poor, was their example as well as
their Savior; and they could be Christians only as they
had the mind which was in Christ.

O, for a breath of this Christ-like Christianity.
O for a gale of it like the mighty rushing wind of old.
Where is it? We ask what a man is worth, and count
the answer by his income. The only Christianity which
Jesus Christ acknowledges is that which treats every
man as brother. The poor man has to love the rich as
well as the rich man love the poor, all men are bound
by the love of God.

We are marked off from all other creatures, not
only by our need of God, but by our need of one another. The rich need sympathy, and they get envy. The
poor, too, need sympathy, and they get it from one another, which the rich do not; but, alas, how often are
they dreaded and scorned and suspected. The great

middle class, certainly the happiest of the three, is exposed to the envy of those below them, and the scorn of those above them; while genius too often sits mocking the wretchedness of all.

Do not wait until things are set right for us, the early disciples certainly did not do that. They believed that they served One who was come — not coming — to set things right; who was manifested already to destroy the works of the devil. Do not wait until we can find some definite plan that commends itself to everybody's judgment. What we have to do is to give ourselves up to Christ for the fulfillment of his great purposes in us and through us. We have in his strength and for his sake to live the life of a Christ-like brotherliness.

Let us consider the poor. Think about them tenderly, resolved to help them as wisely and well as you can. Here, too, does the proverb hold good that necessity is the mother of invention, and the necessities of love alone should come first. God is love; and it is good, as it is true, to think that as every sun ray that touches the earth has the sun at the other end of it, so every bit of love upon God's earth has God at the other end of it. Love, true love, is the only love. Loving, Christ-like, tender considerateness is mainly needed in the world.

One result that would follow immediately from such considerateness is that every church and chapel would have some place open every night, warmed, cheerful, and attractive, as easily got at as the public house, as comfortable as the bar-parlor; where men and women and young people could sit and read without being either lectured or patronized, but welcomed simply as brothers.

Sometime ago I was going down a main thoroughfare of the city in which I then resided, when I saw about thirty men who were at work in some way about the road, laying drains or something of that sort. It was the dinner hour, and there in the pelting rain they sat eating their provision — about as dreary and cheerless a scene as one could see. In that road, within a mile, there were no less than five places of worship, the nearest was that of which I was then the minister. I at once got the school room opened, and bade the men welcome, promised it should be at their service so long as they were anywhere near, and had a fire at which they could warm their coffee and themselves. When their work lay further down the road another place was similarly opened to receive them. Now comes the interesting part of the story. On Sunday some of those men walked a long way and endured a sermon, because, as one explained, "You see, one good turn deserves another." I certainly much appreciated the kindness of that good turn. Those men will henceforth carry a more kindly feeling toward the religion of Jesus Christ. Let us pray earnestly for the Christ-like brotherliness toward men, and opportunities of service will not be lacking.

Another thing which assuredly should be seen to, and that very speedily, is the neglect of the godly poor by the churches. Surely Christ our Master is alike astonished and indignant at the extent to which we lavish money upon the fabric in which we worship him, and leave the poor members of the church to the miseries of pauperism. The church needs to think about consecrating one-tenth of the income to all religious uses. The Jew gave three-tenths, and one-tenth was wholly for the poor. How immediately this Christ-like care for the poor followed upon the baptism of power!

Turn to the 4th chapter of the Acts, 33rd and 34th verses: *"And with great power gave the apostles witness of the resurrection of the Lord Jesus: and great grace was upon them all. Neither was there any among them that lacked; for as many as were possessors of lands or houses sold them, and brought the prices of the things that were sold, and laid them down at the apostles' feet: and distribution was made unto every man according as he had need."* (Acts 4:33 & 34).

The first appointment of officers in the Christian church was to this care of the poor; and the seven deacons were appointed "to serve the tables." How significant is the contrast in Mark's record of how, while the disciples were marveling at the manner of the stones, Jesus was far more interested in a certain poor widow who came bringing her gift to the treasury! The fabric, however costly and beautiful, has little charm for Jesus beside a living, loving heart.

Once, and only once, Christ lifted the veil of the world beyond, it was to reveal one tormented in the "white heat of God's indignation," whose offense was not that he was rich — his sin was that he found life's good in his goods, and not in doing good; and that he left his poor brother at his gate, unpitied, unrelieved.

Chapter XI

WE ARE WITNESSES

"Ye shall receive power, after that the Holy Ghost
is come upon you: and ye shall be witnesses
unto me." (Acts 1:8).

We cannot please ourselves as to whether we
will be witnesses or not. If we make any profession of
faith in Jesus Christ, we are witnesses. The danger is
lest we should be witnesses without the power. Who is
Jesus Christ? He is ever at the bar of public opinion;
and whether men shall accept him, or whether they
shall reject him, depends upon the evidence we give as
to his character. Well might he bid his disciples tarry
until they were endued with power from on high — the
less the world saw of them the better. If we could only
keep all the un-Christ-like Christians out of sight, the
great hindrance to the triumph of the gospel would be

gone. The man who makes a duty of family prayer in the morning, and then gets up to be hard, impatient, angry, makes his Christianity hated. The children and the servants say, "That is religion?" and they ridicule it and they are right, quite right. If the religion of Jesus Christ does not make us gentle and loving and tender, whatever is the good of it? The man who goes to the house of God on Sunday, and is earnest in church work, and then on Monday can be keen in business, inconsiderate of others, hard and grasping, as eager after the world as anybody else, provokes the scorn of the world. It shrugs its shoulder and sneers, "That is your religion?" It would surely be better to tarry at Jerusalem, to be hidden altogether out of sight; for these things do crucify again the Son of God, and put him to an open shame. Surely, it were a thousand times better never to stir in our discipleship until we get the power from on high.

Does this sadden us? More than sadden; it may perhaps altogether dishearten us. It seems to say that unless we are perfect, we had better not be Christians at all. Yet, if we are not to begin until we are perfect, we shall never begin at all. We are his disciples, not because we are good, but because we want to be so.

But, let us turn again to the company of the early disciples. Can you think how each of them would have felt if this purpose of their discipleship had become clear to them, that they were to go forth and live over again the Christ-like life? The full purpose, doubtless, was somewhat veiled from them, but it is easy to think how it would have affected them if only they could have seen it.

I think John rises first, and slowly goes forth from the little company, his face full of grief, and his heart too full for any utterance except in tears — "I could never let men see what He is like," he thinks within himself; "never. Alas, what fires rage in me. Did I not want to call down the judgment of heaven upon those Samaritans? Little wonder that the Master named me 'A Son of Thunder.' How could I ever let men see in me his gentleness, his patience, his tenderness, his love? If only it had been to tell men about him, to work for him, to die for him—that I could have done. But to have in me the mind that was also in him, and to live his life! Would indeed that it were possible!" and again there comes the sigh of despair.

Next follows Thomas; poor Thomas — always somewhat alone, one thinks. He, too, rises very sadly, feeling that he must go. If John can never be a true witness of the Lord Jesus, what, then, shall he do? If he were like the simple-minded Philip, or the outspoken Peter, he might have some hope; but, as it is, he seems the very last man to go forth in such a service.

Then Philip rises, looking about him as if to see what others should do, that he might find some loop-hole of escape, open-eyed and wondering. "Ah me" he thinks, "there is chance for me If I were only good like John, or clever like Thomas, or brave like Peter!" and he sighs to think that he is like nobody but himself. "I seem to have no gifts, and could never, never let men see what he is like." He, too, must go.

Then comes Peter. The tears creep down his face. "A witness to him? to live his life amongst men." Alas, had he not denied his Master thrice, with oaths and curses? He hoped he might have lived to show his Lord that he did love him, but he could never live to show the world what he was like." He must go.

So, one after another, all are going forth. Who could ever count himself fit for such a service—a witness unto him! And you and I, dear reader, must go forth also and let men see his beauty and his worth.

But Jesus looks upon them all, with eyes that read them through and through — John, Thomas, Philip and Simon — and he said "YE." He did not pick and choose amongst them but all shared alike in the great promise. Blessed be God, he looks upon us and knows us through and through, still he says "YE." Handicap is no hindrance to witness bearing; for it is not what we are that is to be considered so much as what the great Lord can make of us. It is not what we have, but what the Lord can put into us, that settles everything. "*Ye shall receive*" — there is our deliverance, there is our hope. Now may we look forth upon the sacredness of our high calling without fear; for we look up, and there is the supply of all our need. "*Ye shall receive*" — speak it over to yourself until the heart begins to feel the force of it. Take your Bible and underline it by way of scoring it on the heart.

My eye fell upon the word receive. This was not my climbing up, but the coming down of that which I needed. This was not a thing wrought out of me by agony and effort, but something put into me like a seed in the earth. "Receive," I said, "of course I can receive." "My Lord, I do bring Thee my poor heart — fill it to the brim." "*Ye shall receive*" — stay your thoughts upon the word until it kindles longing, expectations, the boldness that claims it as your own.

Your Father is the husbandman. He understands this rough stock of our humanity. He knows its evil nature and its little worth. But he knows how to put within it the new nature, the divine. Still there is the old personality; but O, the new unfolding, the sweetness, the beauty, the worth, the glory of it!   "*Ye shall receive*" — not of our struggling or strife does it come; for it is not from within that this grace must spring, but by our surrender to the Father, letting him have his own way perfectly with us in everything. If only we will suffer him to put into us what he can, then shall he get out of us what he wills. Receiving is more than asking, it is claiming and taking. Ask and receive. Be definite and bold in your request. Do not put any wished for experience in the place of faith. Go boldly and ask for this gift of the Holy Spirit, and then come forth saying, "Now, because God has promised, the gift is mine. The manifestation of his indwelling may be gradual, but be assured it shall be. The manifestation of the power may be different from what we are looking for, as it was different from that which these early disciples expected, but this shall infallibly be ours — we shall be witnesses unto him.

How often have men and women without any special genius or great gifts risen up into resistless power for God by the indwelling might of the Spirit? So to us may the promise be fulfilled — "*He that is feeble among them at that day shall be as David.*" (Zechariah 12:8).

All this is for us. Let us receive it.

Chapter XII

THE VICTORY ILLUSTRATED

With the utmost reverence we may say the Holy Spirit accomplishes his work. He is here to convince the world of sin, of righteousness, and of judgment to come; he is here to hurl down the stronghold of sin, but he waits for the consecrated heart. Reader, as your eyes rest on this page, God's Word comes to you, *"Ye shall receive power."* Never can you be clear of responsibility of the offer, whether it is accepted or whether it is rejected.. Think again of God's love to the world. Think again of the claims of Christ's infinite sorrow and shame and agony. Think again of the purposes of your own salvation and now, in his strength, give yourself up to God and claim as your own the fulfillment of his promise — *"Ye shall receive power, after that the Holy Ghost is come upon you: and ye shall be witnesses unto me."* (Acts 1:8).

We have dwelt already upon the difference in the disciples before and after Pentecost; but turn to it again to see what Christ can do for the individual witness.

Back against the door of the Judgment Hall, where he will be least suspected, there sits Peter; back where he can mingle freely with the soldiers who gather round the fire. The fire flings its ruddy glare upon the breastplate and helmet, and now upon this weather-beaten fisherman. A quick-eyed soldier detects him; another catches his dialect, and together they cry, "*Why, thou art one of his disciples.*" (John 18:17). Instantly he denies it. O, shameful denial, and at such a time! Is this his witness?

Now a girl joins the company. The disciple may well have shrunk back where the shadows fall thickest; but holding up a lighted brand, it may be, to let the glare fall full upon him, she cries, "*Thou art one of his disciples.*" (John 18:17). Again the denial, angrily, and with an oath. "*I saw thee with him,*" saith the soldier. "*His speech betrayeth him,*" cries another. "*It is the fellow that cut off my kinsman's ear,*" (John 18:26), clamors a third. And yet again the oath, "I never knew him!" Then in upon the tumult the crowing of the cock; and Jesus turned and looked. O Peter! poor, poor Peter! who of us dare cast the first stone at thee? Well mayest thou hurry out into the darkness and weep bitterly!

Can such an one ever become a witness? Yet to him it is spoken, Ye shall receive power, after that the Holy Ghost is come upon you.

Step into the judgment hall again, this time by day. Here on the bench sits the high priest and his kindred. Now into the crowded court they bring the prisoner. Look at him! Was ever such a hero? Head up, shoulders back, a face that looks about the court as if he knew not what fear meant; no quailing eye, no quivering lip, but bold as a lion he stands before the judge. They hear the evidence against him, and now they consult as to the sentence; and as the court is silenced, the lord chief justice speaks: "*Prisoner, we charge thee straitly that thou speak no more in the name of Jesus of Nazareth.*" (Acts 5:40). Flinging up the hands and making the chains clank again, he cries, "*Whether it be right in the sight of God to hearken unto you more than unto God, judge ye. For we cannot but speak the things which we have seen and heard.*" (Acts 5:29)

Who is it, this man of splendid courage?

Peter, Simon Peter.

What! He who crept inside the judgment hall, and swore he never knew this Jesus?

The very same.

What has happened to him? He seems very different.

Different! he is indeed. Why, he has received the power from on high, and that has made him so true a witness for Christ.

To thee it is spoken, and to me — "*Ye shall receive power, after that the Holy Ghost is come upon you: and ye shall be witnesses unto ME.*" (Acts 1:8).

Chapter XIII

A WARNING TO THE CHURCH

"Quench not the Spirit."
(1 Thessalonians 5:19)

We have dwelt much upon the purpose of Christ concerning the church, and the promise by which he would fulfill that purpose — "Ye shall receive power, after that the Holy Ghost is come upon you." (Acts 1:8).

The Holy Spirit is come. But there is another and very terrible possibility; instead of our being filled with power, we may turn from all this, and we may quench the Spirit.

The words are to the church. We may have thought of them only as a warning to the unconverted; but if we turn to the beginning of the Epistle we find that it is written *"to the church which is in God the Father, and in the Lord Jesus Christ."* (1 Thessalonians 1:1).

"We give thanks to God always for you all. . . . Remembering without ceasing your work of faith, and labor of love, and patience of hope in our Lord Jesus Christ, in the sight of God and our Father; knowing, brethren beloved, your election of God. For our gospel came not unto you in word only, but also in power, and in the Holy Ghost, and in much assurance . . . So that ye were examples to all that believe." (1 Thessalonians 1:3). Then as he came near to the end of this letter he writes these words, *"Quench not the Spirit."* (1 Thessalonians 5:19).

Is it not to the church that the most terrible words of this book are spoken? When Jesus came he had pity for the outcast; he bent over the harlots; he welcomed the prodigals; he prayed for his murderers; but there were some to whom he could only speak words of black and hopeless condemnation; and they were members of the church — the religious people, the very religious indeed. They were religious all day long; they were religious in everything; they would not eat a meal but their religion came into it — religious in their washing, religious in their dressing, religious in their looks, yet these were the people whom Christ greeted as a generation of vipers, and himself wondered how they could escape the damnation of hell. So it was in the time of Isaiah. To the people who came to prayer, and who brought sacrifice and offered incense, God spoke words of terrible reproof — *"When ye spread forth your hands, I will hide mine eyes; when ye make many prayers, I will not hear."* (Isaiah 1:15).

What then, is it better to be a drunkard, a harlot, a murderer, than to be a Christian? Well, yes, it is, unless your Christianity makes you like Jesus Christ. The greatest responsibility in this world is the responsibility of knowing Christ; and, there is no condemnation so terrible as that which rests upon the man who has had all the privileges and promises and opportunities of Christianity at his disposal, and yet he has turned them to no account.

There is no genius, no position, no gift which will ever bring upon any man such responsibility as this of knowing Christ. God has shown us his love in the unspeakable gift of his Son, he has given to us the Holy Spirit, he has given to us the Word with its visions and promises, He has revealed to us what he would have us to be. Now, whether on the one hand, we respond to these gracious invitations, or whether on the other hand, we sink down content with hearing of them and desiring them, God holds us responsible, not for what we have, but for what we might have — not for what we are, but for what we might be. It is by God's offers and by our opportunities that we shall be judged and by which we shall be condemned, by that truer and fuller and higher life into which the Holy Spirit has come to lead us.

The work of the Holy Spirit which exposes us to this peril of quenching the Spirit is manifest again and again in the Epistles of Paul. Turn, for instance to the Epistle written to the Ephesians. He does not once pray for them that their sins may be forgiven, but he starts from that point. *"After I heard of your faith in the Lord Jesus Christ, and love unto all the saints, I cease not to*

*give thanks for you, making mention of you in my prayers,
that the God of our Lord Jesus Christ, the Father of glory,
may give unto you the spirit of wisdom and revelation in the
knowledge of him: the eyes of your heart being enlightened
that ye may know what is the hope of his calling, and what
the riches of the glory of his inheritance in the saints."*
(Ephesians 1:15). That we may see what we may be —
that is the great work of the Holy Spirit in the church,
and to lead us up to it. We are apt to make the hope of
our calling a poor, low, outside thing — an escape, not
from ill-temper and selfishness and indolence and pride,
but only an escape from hell; not a power which is to
make us like God and ready for his service, but only to
take us to heaven when we die. This is our natural
tendency, to be content with religion without Christ-
likeness, that which is so terribly denounced by the Lord
Jesus. Now the Holy Spirit is come to open up to us
glorious possibilities. He reveals to us sunny vistas and
delicious retreats where we may sit in the heavenly
places with Christ. He lifts the clouds and we look up
the mountain side, and a gracious voice bids us "Come
up higher." What we will make of all these revelations
and promptings depends upon ourselves. We may give
ourselves up to the Spirit's leadings, and then, then only,
are we the sons of God. He will not drag us; he will not
force us; but if we are willing to go with him, listening
for his voice, and giving up our whole soul to his guid-
ance, then shall he bring us into the large and wealthy
place. Or we may hear of these things, and be content
with vague wishes and idle dreams, and lie with but
bare memories of what was begun in us, forever poor,
forever feeble, the great possibilities of God's grace all

unknown; and the treasures which might have enriched and blessed men, all unexplored and unpossessed.

Let us ask ourselves very earnestly, how may we quench the Spirit? It is startling to find the suggestion which immediately follows these words, "*Despise not prophesyings.*" (1 Thessalonians 5:20). Nothing could be so certain to quench the Spirit as the spirit of scorn. Of the three steps downward to perdition, neglecting, rejecting, despising — the last is indeed the last; beyond it can only be the blackness of darkness. He that rejecteth, rejecteth not man, but God, who gives us his Holy Spirit. Even as there is no surer way of putting out a fire than by pouring cold water on it, there is no surer way of quenching the Spirit than by rejecting and despising his revelations and promptings.

Holiness is sneered at as the sentimental dream of weak-minded people. God has called us, and is calling us, unto holiness; he that despises, despises not man, but God who has given us the Holy Spirit.

"He that rejects" — "*Quench not the Sprit*" — "*Despise not.*" (1 Thessalonians 5:19). The words set vividly before us the figure of Esau, who despised his birthright, and for a mess of pottage bartered the high calling and his relationship to the Christ. By his indulgence, he let go the golden future and all its glory and high privilege.

We profess to be Christ's soldiers and servants, purchased by his blood and going onward into his presence; yet, we do not make his service the great purpose of our life; we do not surrender everything to it. That place is kept for business or some pleasure. When society, gain, honor, position, or pleasures have more charm for us than the presence and good pleasure of our Savior Jesus Christ — is that not to despise our birthright, and to be like Esau of old?

The surest way of quenching the Spirit is to have some secret sin, or some silly fear or some gain or pleasure. There is no lie so utterly ruinous to a man as habitually to live false to the light of God, false to one's better self; to keep that better self as Herod kept John the Baptist, in the dungeon. There is no surer way of undermining the whole moral nature, so that when the moment of decision and trial comes, as it comes to every man, the power of resistance is gone, and the man is swept away, an utter and hopeless wreck. "*Quench not the Spirit*" — "*Despise not.*" (1 Thessalonians 5:19-20).

Another way of putting out the fire of God and quenching the Spirit is to let it alone. Many have time only for wishes. It is not an accident that makes the proverb associate the folly of wishes with idle beggars. There is no more miserable way of cheating the soul than contenting ourselves with desire. There is nothing promised to wishes. "*Ask, and it shall be given; seek, and ye shall find; knock, and it shall be opened.*" (Matthew 7:7). Seeking, expecting, claiming, these are the steps up to possession. Beware of this habit. Satan tempts men on to indulgence in it like a narcotic, it soothes and stupefies the soul, and quenches the Spirit.

Yet, again, we often put out the fire of God with shovelfuls of rubbish. Many will say, "Well, you know, I am not like other people — I am very peculiar; I do not understand, or I cannot feel." They pile up their complaints and failings, and they put the fire out. O, this dreadful rubbish! Our weakness, our folly, our peculiarities, are no hindrances to him, and the greater the hindrances are to us, the more reason there is that we should come to God for help. If we will give ourselves up to him, he can do as much for us as he ever did for any. It is an insult, indeed, a sin and a shame, when the Holy Spirit of God comes to lead us on to these higher things, that we should limit his grace and power by our failings and weaknesses. He is come to help such foolish and weak ones as ourselves. No wonder the Holy Spirit is grieved, insulted quenched.

Are you where God would have you to be? If not, come out, and right away at once; for you certainly ought not to be there. If you are, then be afraid to complain of circumstances which God has ordained on purpose to work out in you the very image and likeness of his Son.

There is not resting place between these two — the great purpose of God fulfilled; the Holy Spirit received by us, and we made witnesses unto Christ, or the Holy Spirit quenched. The words came to us from God; let them arouse and alarm and urge us to the full surrender of ourselves to him. *"Quench not the Spirit."* (1 Thessalonians 5:19).

Chapter XIV

PHARISAISM

"He began to say unto his disciples first of all,
Beware ye of the leaven of the Pharisees."
(Luke 12:1).

Leaven of the Pharisees — it seems a mistaken phrase. We do not wonder that the disciples were perplexed as to the Master's meaning. Pharisaism, surely, is not much like leaven. Leaven is little, leaven is hidden, leaven is noiseless; whereas, Pharisaism is the very opposite of all that. Pharisaism was pompous, with Pharisaism, to be seen of men was the beginning of its existence. Its dress stood out with a very vivid distinctness, its prayers were long and loud at the street corners, its alms were trumpeted, its presence was greeted with sounding phrases and stately courtesies. But the

Master, who searches hearts, saw its subtlest spirit, and looking underneath the particular manifestations of it, name it rightly leaven.

"*He began to say unto his disciples first of all, beware ye of the leaven of the Pharisees.*" The Pharisees were a distinct sect, in every way wholly distinct from these poor fishermen. The Pharisees were the proudest and most exclusive circle of all the proud Jews of Judea, walking the earth with a strut as if they had conferred an honor by condescending to be born in it, sunning themselves as if the great luminary had risen expressly for the honor of seeing such sublime specimens of humanity. What had these simple fishermen to do with such high lords? The Master seems twice to have spoken these words of warning; and, the second time they turned to one another, wondering as to his meaning, until they whispered: "*He means that we have forgotten to take bread.*" Jesus rebuked their blindness. "*O ye of little faith, do ye not remember the five loaves of the five thousand, and how many baskets ye took up; and the seven loaves of the four thousand, and how many baskets ye took up? Then understood they how that he bade them not beware of the leaven of bread, but of the doctrine of the Pharisees.*" (Matthew 16:5). But the explanation explained little. He bade them beware. What had they to do with the Pharisees? A great social gulf yawned between them, which none could cross. All their associations rose up as a bulwark between them. How could they possibly catch the infection of Pharisaism? They did not breathe the same air, scarcely lived in the same world.

Is it not ever thus? The Pharisee — it seems the easiest thing in the world to sketch the character, so that in a moment everything within us shall flame in fury against these hypocrites. Yet is there one thing easier, and that is ourselves, to be defiled by the leaven. The easiest thing in the world is to belong to the Pharisees — perhaps the very hardest thing in the world is to know it. *"Take heed ye, and beware of the leaven of the Pharisees."* (Matthew 16:6). It is, as the Master said, a leaven — a subtle thing that lurks within, working its mischief unsuspected.

The words reach back to a scene which gives them yet a greater fullness of meaning. The Pharisees, unable to trap Jesus in their public encounters with him, seek now for a more private interview, and one of them asks Jesus to share the morning meal at his house. Now he sits with the gaze of unfriendly faces watching him. At the outset they are horrified at seeing him take bread without first washing his hands. Their miserable formalism had exalted it into an act of supreme religiousness. They held that it was better to kill a man than to commit such a crime as that. They are the more indignant because the offense was aggravated in every possible way. The Pharisee always bathed himself whenever he came from the market, to wash away the defiling contact of the common people; and, Jesus had been pressed by a multitude so great that we read of them as having trodden upon one another in their eagerness to get near him. He had cast out devils, and in many ways had come in contact with the unclean. The guests turn to each other with eyes that flash in anger at this outrage. Jesus at once avails himself of the opportunity:

"Ye Pharisees make clean the outside of the cup and the platter: but your inward part is full of ravening and wickedness. Ye fools, did not He that made the outside make the inside also? . . . Woe unto you Pharisees! for ye tithe mint and rue and every herb, and pass over judgment and the love of God. . . . Woe unto you Pharisees! for ye love the uppermost seats in the synagogues, and greetings in the markets. . . . Woe unto you, lawyers, also, for ye load men with burdens grievous to be borne, and ye yourselves touch not the burdens with one of your fingers! Woe unto you! for ye build the tombs of the prophets, and your fathers killed them, . . . that the blood of all the prophets which was shed from the foundation of the world might be required of this generation, from the blood of Abel to the blood of Zechariah, who perished between the alter and the temple."

"And as he said these things unto them, the scribes and the Pharisees began to urge him vehemently, and to provoke him to speak many things; lying in wait for him, and seeking to catch something out of his mouth, that they might accuse him." (Luke 11:39-54).

Doubtless the indignation spread to the disciples. John's eyes flash indignant fires. Peter can scarcely restrain his fury, and every face is full of tenderest pity for their dear Lord and Master thus beset and assailed and thus moved to indignation. Now that unhappy time is ended. He comes forth again. Once more he breathes the air of heaven, once more he meets the honest faces of his disciples. We listen for a sigh of relief, when, lo! he looks eagerly upon his simple followers, and says to them first of all, *"Beware ye — ye of the leaven of the Pharisees."* (Matthew 16:6)

"*Beware ye*" — every sect of religion, every variety of character has its own danger — perhaps its own form of Pharisaism. It is easy for us to see the Pharisaism of others. We can stone the Pharisee in an indignant zeal—and what then? When the storm is over, and we have hurled the lightnings, there stands the Master, with eyes that search us through, and he bends over us, and saith unto his disciples, first of all, "*Beware ye of the leaven of the Pharisees.*" (Matthew 16:6). We too may have our own form of Pharisaism eating the life out of us; spoiling all the beauty and blessedness of our religion. To those that are nearest and dearest to him this word is spoken by the Lord himself.

What then is Pharisaism? We shall mistake the whole meaning of the words if we think only of the coarse hypocrite, who knows within himself that he is a fraud, wearing a cloak of piety only to hide his own foul purposes. Judas was a hypocrite, but he was in no sense a Pharisee. The Pharisees believed themselves to be really good people, the only good people, the exalted favorites of God, the very heirs of heaven. The caution will lose its force if we think only of the man who knows that his whole life is a lie. Pharisaism is a far subtler thing than that. Pharisaism is a poison germ that can only be developed in religion. Here we find it in a religion that controlled everything — a religion that was very earnest and very sincere. With the Pharisee, religion was his one supreme thought and pursuit. Bring your tests of a religious life and apply them here. Does it pray? Indeed it does, with the unfailing regularity of stated periods, a clear half hour by the clock. Does it search the Scriptures? Yes, indeed, it has the Bible at its finger ends, and studies nothing else, carrying out its directions in the minutest particulars. Does it give freely? That is reckoned a good sign. Is the pocket converted? Yes, indeed a most exact and measured tenth, down to its parsley and peppermint. Does it go to church? With a splendid regularity, it is a very pattern of reverent devotion. Yet, Christ hurls at it the most terrible denunciations that ever fell from his lips. There is one other test that we can apply, and this Pharisaism is at once betrayed wherever it lurks. Does this religion make its professor Christ-like?

There is its doom — beliefs held with a jealous orthodoxy, but without any living faith. Prayer regularly offered, but without any living communion with the Father in heaven. Scriptures read, but without any aspiration after true holiness. Abundant in charity giving, but without any touch of brotherly kindness, without a breath of generosity. Religious, very religious indeed, yet an utter stranger to all meekness and graciousness and self-forgetfulness. That is Pharisaism; religion without Christ-likeness.

Is this not the supreme want of the age, as indeed of all the ages? Alas, that it should seem so far off! We have churches, chapels, hymns, prayers, missions, conferences, sermons, in bewildering abundance — but how wanting is the power that makes men Christ-like!

All things work to this one end — that we be conformed to the image of his Son. If we have not his Spirit, we are none of his. If this likeness to our Lord be lacking, in vain we plead our beliefs, our prayers, our raptures, our associations, our gifts. From within the closed doors there comes the answer, grieved, yet unalterable, I never knew you. So rings the dreadful doom of the religion that stops short of Christ-likeness.

Let us search out, if it be possible, the cause of this failure. Take Saul of Tarsus, afterwards Paul, as a specimen first of the Pharisee, and afterwards of the true Christian. *"I am a Pharisee, the son of a Pharisee,"* he says of himself. *"and after the most strait sect of our religion I live a Pharisee."* (Acts 23:6). He was not, therefore, a hypocrite. No, indeed; zealous beyond any, as truly conscientious and ardent in his Pharisaism as afterwards in his Christianity. Now he becomes a Christian. What is the great difference in the man? Before and after his knowing Christ he is alike earnest, devout, zealous. When did the Pharisee die and the Christian begin? It is here — the center of the old life was "I," the center of the new life is Christ. Pharisaism is a capital "I," a very religious "I," finding in religion that which magnifies and exalts its importance. We hear it in the prayer, if prayer it can be called: *"Lord, I thank thee that I am not as other men. I fast twice in the week; I give tithes of all that I possess."* (Luke 18:11). The consciousness that runs through it all is that same "I" and so, of course, all things and all persons are measured by that same "I." He that does not worship as I worship is a heretic; excommunicate him. He that does not think as I think is an offender, stone him. That is the essence of Pharisaism.

But the moment Paul finds Christ there is a new consciousness, a new center, there is a new grammar in which "I" becomes the second person singular, and "thou" is ever the first person. The first step in his Christian life is an absolute surrender of himself to Jesus

Christ. "*Lord, what wilt thou have me to do?*" (Acts 9:6). The gospel according to Paul was not meant first of all for deliverance, but for surrender. "*I have been crucified with Christ; yet I live; and yet no longer I, but Christ liveth in me; and that life which I now live in the flesh I live in faith, the faith which is in the Son of God who loved me, and gave himself for me.*" (Galatians 2:20). Now, forever beats and throbs within him the consciousness of belonging to Christ. I, Paul, the slave of the Lord Jesus Christ, is the utterance that rises to his lips at every reference to himself.   Christianity meant Paul's own death and burial, that henceforth Christ might be enthroned in his heart and glorified by every thought and word and deed of his life. That first, and then alongside of that, and growing out of it, a passionate longing for the welfare of those about him.

Turning from Paul to yet a nobler example, wherein lay the great difference between Jesus himself and the Pharisees, whom he so sternly denounced. Each was very religious, each was fervent, intense, devout. What was it that severed them and put them as wide apart as heaven and hell? It was this — the life of the Lord Jesus Christ was an utter surrender of himself, always and in everything, to the will of God and to the good of men. "*My meat is to do the will of him that sent me.*" (John 4:34). "*I seek not mine own will of the Father which hath sent me.*" (John 5:30). "*Not my will, but thine be done.*" (Luke 22:42). Besides this surrender of the will, and growing out of it, was the surrender of himself for the lives of men. "*I lay down my life for the brethren.*" (John 10:15). There is the distinction which forever severs the two, the essence and leaven of Pharisaism is

"I", the essence and strength of Christianity is self-surrender to the glory of God and to the good of others.

How does this curse of Pharisaism poison the religious life of today? Look at it in our knowledge of Christ. To us it may seem an amazing thing that these Pharisees of old could come into contact with the Lord Jesus Christ, and yet never be conscious of his sublime goodness, that unblemished beauty of holiness, that great love which wrapped a world in its embrace, that lofty courage which never faltered in the face of all the terrible foes which threatened him, that all this should never have arrested them, never have awed them. Pilate sees Jesus, and is afraid of the sufferer, so meek and so majestic. The centurion bends low before the crucified, and whispers with a troubled fear; *"Truly this was the Son of God."* (Mark 15:39). The common people heard him gladly, and publicans and sinners declared that "man never spoke like this Man." This is ever the curse of Pharisaism — this utter darkness. No love is so blind as self-love. It is stone blind, stone deaf, stone dead to all but its own little advantage.

"Then said he to his disciples first of all, beware ye of the leaven of the Pharisees." (Matthew 16:6).

Why do we marvel at their blindness? Are there not in our midst thousands and tens of thousands who know all about Jesus Christ; who know him in the glorious completeness of his love; who know the story of his birth, his life, his death, his resurrection? Yet he himself is no vision of beauty, after whom the heart goes out in eager admiration; and his presence is no delight. There are thousands who kneel before him as Lord, and who seek his blessing, and whose hope of forgiveness rest in him, yet their lives are utterly self-centered. "I think," and "I like," and "I shall" — this is supreme as ever. Their very religion ministers only and solely to the capital "I." They have never seen self as a thing condemned, a thing to be crucified, dead, buried, put away forever, that the new Man, the Lord from heaven, may come in to reign within them. Our remedy is only in escaping from self to Jesus Christ. It is in receiving him, and beholding him, and communing with him, and delighting in him, until self is forgotten in the abiding presence of Jesus Christ; and, Jesus himself becomes more and more the very center of our being — the new and better self who lives in us.

Chapter XV

THE CHRISTIANITY OF
JESUS CHRIST:
HOW MAY IT BE OURS?

"Be perfect, be of good comfort."
(2 Corinthians 8:11)

A glance at the words is enough to make us feel how contradictory they are. Be perfect — that is a word that strikes us with despair. At once we feel how far away we are from our own poor ideal; and, alas, how much further from God's ideal concerning us! *"Be perfect"* (2 Corinthians 13:11). — it seems to take us by the hand and to point us up some slippery height, which only very skillful mountaineers have ever climbed, — and have we not heard that those who reach the top are in great peril of speedily slipping down again? We have to get up there; and to stay there! Is it any good our trying?

131

"*Be of good comfort*" (2 Corinthians 13:11) — ah, that is very different. That seems to say: "Do not fret; do not fear." If you are not what you would be, you must be thankful for what you are. Certainly you might be better, but as certainly you might be worse, and in these things we must strike the average.

Now the question is this, How can these two be reconciled? How keep up any aspiration after perfection amid so many conscious failures — still more, how amidst such failures keep up the aspiration with a cheery confidence? This is the sublime achievement of Christianity. Other systems of religion have held these precepts separately. Great heathen systems, of which we should speak with reverent honor, have said, "*Be perfect;*" but it has been by agony, by torture, by endless processes of self-extinction. They have left out the other part — "*Be of good comfort.*" Many systems have cried, "Be of good comfort — eat, drink, tomorrow we die;" but they have had no place for the other words — "*Be perfect.*" It is only the religion of Jesus Christ that reconciles these two. He stands in our midst, and with the right hand of his righteousness he points us upward, and says, "*Be perfect.*" There is no resting place short of that. Yet with the left hand of his love he does encompass us, as he says, "soul, be of good comfort;" or, "that is what I am come to do for thee."

Many people lose both their perfection and their comfort because they put them in the wrong order. They put "*be of good comfort*" first, and then they let the "*be perfect*" find its way behind as it can. Their test and proof of religion is feeling happy. There are many young people in our congregations to whom this is the one thought — the end and aim of religion, to make them happy. They go home on a Sunday evening after a stirring sermon, and say, "Well, I think I am saved tonight, I feel happier;" but, tomorrow the happiness is gone, and they give up again in despair. With many a man, feeling is the gauge by which he tests his spiritual condition. The beginning and the end of his religion is this, to be made happy.

There are tens of thousands with whom this is the one great hindrance to the possession of the Christianity of Jesus Christ — so that there is much need to consider the matter carefully and on all sides. Let us look at the matter boldly. Is the great end and purpose of our religion to make us feel happy?

Surely it is a pitiable and unworthy ideal of life. Come into Westminster Abbey, and let us read the memorials of the mighty dead. Who are these that the nation delights to honor? Here are the warriors who went forth to meet troops of discomforts, and death himself in a hundred shapes. Did they feel happy? No, indeed, when bullets were whistling past them, and cannon balls came uncomfortably close, and the shells burst about them; but, what had they to do with feeling happy? They had to do their duty or to die in trying — they did it, the one or the other; and the nation said these men were heroes.

Turn to your Arctic explorers again, having all sorts of misery and death in many shapes. There was not much happiness for them, hemmed in by the gloom and fierceness of an Arctic winter; but, what had they to do with feeling happy? The glory of the men was that they counted not their lives dear to them in the doing of their duty. Happy? No indeed, not as they think of the wife and little ones at home.

Think of philanthropists and martyrs, who have lived and toiled and suffered and died to bless their fellow men, whose life has been an incessant toil and a perpetual sacrifice. Amongst these shall we set a highly respectable tombstone, and inscribe upon it the record, "Here lies a man who felt happy." Noble person — who got up in the morning, and ate and drank, and bought and sold, and slept, and touched this lofty purpose of being — he felt happy! If that is the highest end and purpose of my religion, I can find an altogether nobler ideal of life elsewhere.

If this is the purpose of religion, surely our Lord Jesus Christ has come the wrong way. Can we think of anything that could make us more completely and perfectly miserable than an attempt to secure our own happiness by the anguish of another? If I were a homeless wanderer, hungry, wretched, ragged, perishing, and unable to go a step farther in the bleak winds and piercing cold, and I sink at your doorstep — what if you should come forth and lay your hand upon my shoulder, and bid me come in and sit by the fire, and eat your supper, and rest in your chair; and, you would go forth to take my place in the bitter cold. Do you think I should feel happy? Never. I tell you your fire would scorch me, your supper would choke me, the comforts would be less bearable than my previous discomforts, and I should come forth and say, "Sir, either you will come in and share my good things, or I will come forth and share your evil things. I am not such a mean creature as to be made happy at a cost like this!"

"Ah, my Lord, you have spoiled my happiness. I take your hand, and I feel that dreadful wound-print. I look into your face, and I track that cruel crown of thorns. I rest against your side, and I remember how it was pierced and torn for me. My Lord, take me and lift me up, let me hang with you upon the cross, that I may say, I am crucified with Christ. My happiness is spoiled by the pain and agony and shame and awful curse of Calvary."

There is no great virtue in feeling happy. I do not know that I could be much more confident of any man's honesty because he assured me that he felt happy; or that I could rely upon his word with more assurance on that account. I suppose a drunken man feels happy, or surely he would never pay so hideous a price for it. The Prodical felt happy, no doubt, when he was spending his substance in riotous living in the far country. Or here is a very picture of it — a sky of deepest blue, the woods ablaze with tints of autumn splendor, the acorns and the beech nuts strew the leafy ground, and here lie the swine that have filled themselves with the husks — stretched in the sunshine. Take the picture and write under it the title "*Feeling Happy.*"

If the boy has told a lie, what do you think? Shall I call him, and as he comes, ashamed and afraid, with quivering lip and tearful eye, shall I lightly tell him not to mind? I want him to be happy — that is the great end of life; let him bring his games and shout at his play, and fill the air with his glad laughter. No indeed — everything within us cries aloud and indignantly, "such happiness is a curse." Better pain, shame, grief — anything that should make him feel right down

through him that a lie is an utterly hateful and dam-
nable thing. If my religion is to make me comfortable
in spite of ill temper, and slipshod ways of business, and
words that are not exactly true — then I say deliberately, better the very fires of hell than that comfort, if
they could only burn into and through me a great ab-
horrence of all that is evil.

O, we have not learned the first lesson of Christ's
holy religion, the meaning of the cross has not begun to
dawn upon us, if we have not learned to see in it how
God feels toward sin — that sin is a thing so horrible
and accursed that only in all the awful scene of Calvary
can we see it rightly. He must nail it to the cross, and
thrust it through with a spear, and bury it out of his
sight. It means that sin has so defiled and cursed us
that God can find no remedy for us except in our being
crucified with Christ, dead with Christ, buried with
Christ; that the new Man, the Christ be formed in us,
and that we live now only in the power of his resurrection. The word that runs through the Bible is not first
of all happiness. The whole idea of the Bible — every
command, every promise, every example, all the revelation of God, of heaven, of hell, all the life and sorrows and death of Jesus Christ, every breath and influence of it — teaches me that I want something very
different from feeling comfortable.

Running through the Bible is another word —
a word that needs to be written in letters of fire right
across our churches, and over our shops and factories,
a word that we want stamped upon every product of
our manufactures — the Christian trade-mark, we want
it printed at the head of every ledger and wages book,

we want all transactions weighed by it and measured by it, we want all our words tried by it, we want all the gold and silver rung on this counter. RIGHTEOUS-NESS — that is the word. *"Seek ye first the kingdom of God, and his righteousness."* (Matthew 6:33). *" T h e kingdom of God is not meat and drink, but righteousness."* (Romans 14:17). David, parched and thirsty though he was, poured forth the draught of water from Bethlehem's well an offering unto God, it was a thing which the peril of his brave men had made too sacred for his own indulgence. Christ has shamed us by his own agony and curse out of all thought of our own comfort. He who was rich stooping to all the rude discomforts of poverty, he who is the King of Glory emptying himself and becoming a slave, the Lord and Giver of Life yielding himself to death, even the death of the cross, he — pierced and torn and smitten, — dead. What for? There is but one end and purpose that can warrant such grief and agony as his, that is our holiness. *"First, Be perfect."*

It is precisely here that many earnest persons fail in the religious life — not for want of trying, but for want of the right aim. It is an easy and pleasant thing to travel at the rate of sixty miles and hour when the engine is on the lines; but, when it is off the lines three miles an hour is very difficult, and exceedingly uncomfortable. Many are most conscious of failure, and how can it be otherwise? If God be for us we can-not fail; but, if we move against his will and his way, how can we succeed? If I fall across the machinery of some huge factory it is very likely to rend me; but, if, on the other hand, I fit in with it, and adapt myself to it, all the great forces shall wait upon me and minister to me. Is there, then, any unity in God's great universe — any one definite aim to which everything is adjusted, and up to which all things are working? Can I find out what it is, and can I fit in with it?

"*All things work together;*" here, then, is the first part of my question answered. "*All things*" — the material world, the great sun, the air, the endless life, the very stones and dust of earth, all things — gain, loss, pleasure, pain, the daily worries, the passing pleasure, — all things have one great purpose running through them.

"*All things work together for good.*" (Romans 8:28). God has only got one good. He keeps that word for one thing only. All goods cannot make God's good. This alone is what he counts good — "*That we may be conformed to the image of his Son.*" (Romans 8:29).

All things that I can ever have to do with are set to this one end — to make me like Jesus Christ. The grace of God is the provision by which I am to be adjusted and held rightly towards all things. Now if, at the beginning of the day, I surrender myself to God, not to be taken care of, and fed and clothed, and prospered in business, and made happy, but to be made like Jesus Christ, then I am on the lines. If I will claim the grace of the Holy Spirit to hold myself rightly towards all things, I shall keep my eyes on Jesus. Then shall loss and gain, pain and pleasure, good and ill, be estimated, not by any material worth, but by their contribution to the character, by conformity to Jesus Christ. If gain leave me more eager for the world and more covetous, then gain is an awful loss. If success bring pride and self-importance, then success is a dreadful failure. If pleasures dim and deaden my sense of God's presence, and check my communion with him, then my pleasure is truly an anguish. This is the only end, the test, the proof of our religion — Does it make us like Jesus Christ?

"*First, be perfect;*" and then, "*be of good comfort.*" But while many lose both by the wrong order, some lose both by leaving out the "*Be of good comfort.*" They have heard the word "*Be perfect,*" and all the heart has leaped in response to the appeal. They have felt through and through them that the religion of Jesus Christ is only worthy of him or of us when it sets forth so lofty an ideal, that of all things it is most miserable when the very religion which should for ever destroy our selfishness, itself makes us more selfish. Within us is a deep and abiding instinct that the religion of Jesus can find its aim and end in nothing else that this — Christ-likeness.

But here is the possibility of another peril. Our hearts have cried, "Be perfect! That shall be the one thing for which we will seek and strive until it is ours." Probably we go away and begin by consecrating ourselves to the Lord. We lay ourselves, and the family, and the character, and the possessions, all upon the altar. We tell the Lord we are going to give it all to him, and keep it all for him. Then, with this great burden of our consecrated substance piled up on our shoulders, we set out to climb up the steep and slippery height of perfection! Is it any wonder that very soon the dreadful struggle breaks down utterly, and we sink in despair? Suspicious of every motive, trying to bring every thought and aim into the fierce white light of the Judgment

Throne, questioning everything, doubting and bewildered, condemned at every turn — that, indeed, is to leave out the *"Be of good comfort."*

Do we not see at a glance that all this struggling means that we are bringing in "I" to make "I" perfect? The moment I bring in this "I," that moment I bring in failure. If there is no other way than that, let us not weary and worry ourselves about it.

I cannot consecrate myself to the Lord. My purpose falters and fails in changing circumstances and I am fickle, forgetful, false. My lofty desires of today, tomorrow cease to soar, and sink beneath the clouds again, and rest once more with wearied wings indifferent upon the earth. The only consecration possible is not with me or my will. It is the entrance of the Lord himself, his possessing and claiming and using me, that is the only true consecration. It is not my giving so much as my receiving; not my surrender to him so much as my acceptance of him, on which my mind is to be stayed.

But this agonized effort to make ourselves perfect is not always a failure. Taking hold of rebel self, another part of the self says, "Now I am going to make you perfect." "Self" chips and hammers at "self" to bring it into shape, and hacks and hews at "self" until it fits into the ideal mold. Then it is polished with much sulfuric acid and sandpaper, with what result? At last there is turned out the most unhappy thing that it has ever been our misfortune to meet — from five to six feet of polished "I." All the thought, all the desire, all the aim of life has been set upon "self." Now this same perfected "I" becomes the standard by which everything is measured, and to which everybody must conform, or there is no hope for them in this world or any other. This, as we have seen, is Pharisaism. If this is perfection, the best prayer we can offer is to be saved from it for ever and ever. Thank God, that is not his way of holiness.

"*Be perfect, be of good comfort.*" (2 Corinthians 13:11). Do we not feel that if ever we are going to be that which in our best moments we want to be, it must begin in "self" lost, "self" forgotten, "self" not so much denied as "self" ignored, unheeded? This is exactly what is meant by the word which the Lord Jesus used when he bade the disciple deny himself.

"*Be perfect.*" My faith in perfection is very weak when I look at others, it is extinguished altogether when I look at myself. But, when I look at Jesus, I can believe in nothing else. He is perfect in all his works, and no other aim than this can ever satisfy him. The work which he has undertaken to do for us would not bear his stamp if it stopped anywhere short of perfection; and, for such a vast expenditure and cost I dare not think of anything less than this. When he comes, what limit shall I set to his grace? So, as I stand looking up that slippery height, wondering how its summit is to be reached, he comes with his gracious words — "My child, fear not! What you are seeking is not by climbing up, it is in my coming down. *Be perfect.*"

The only perfection of which I can think is spelled with five letters — JESUS. This, and this only, is holiness — Jesus received, Jesus communed with, Jesus welcomed, Jesus served, Jesus pleased in all the temper and spirit of life. It is not in my understanding theories or theologies, not in my perception of methods, not in my experience of raptures or agonies, but in Jesus Christ received into the heart that he may do his own work in his own way. Look up to him now. Claim him and welcome him as your own, able and eager to do as much for you as he ever did for any. Hold him within your heart where he seeks to make his home.

He that hath ears to hear, let him hear. With eye and heart and hope and longing fixed upon Jesus Christ our Lord, he himself bends over us, he shines upon us, he looses, he uplifts. How, it is not for us to know or care; but, this we do know —

WE ARE TRANSFORMED BY BEHOLDING.

Additional copies of
**The Christianity of Jesus Christ,
Is It Ours?**
by Mark Guy Pearse
may be ordered from First Century
Publishing
1-800-578-6060
or online at
www.firstcenturypublishing.com
$12.95 USA

Devoted to Christian Publications,

First Century Publishing
P.O. Box 130
Delmar, NY 12054
(518) 439-3544 / Fax: (518) 439-0105